Recollections of Victorian Birmingham

Stephen Roberts

Published under the imprint *Birmingham Biographies*

Printed by CreateSpace

© Stephen Roberts, 2018

All rights reserved. No part of this publication may be reproduced in any form, stored in or re-introduced into a retrieval system, or transmitted, in any form or by any means, electronic, mechanical, photocopying, recording or otherwise without the prior consent of the author.

The moral right of Stephen Roberts to be identified as the author of this work has been asserted in accordance with the Copyright, Designs and Patents Act 1988.

ISBN-13: 978-1719078887

ISBN-10: 1719078882

Front cover: Omnibuses in High Street, Birmingham, in 1869. From the editor's collection

To the memory of Pete James

Contents

Contents i
Acknowledgements ii
Preface iii
Recollections of Victorian Birmingham 1

    Charles Lee 1
    'An Octogenarian' 4
    Edward Preston 7
    Alfred Davenport 10
    John Deeley 12
    John Suffield 14
    'An Old Architect' 17
    William Downing 21
    T.H. Aston 24
    F.W. Humphreys 26
    Samuel Edmonds 28
    Henry Moorhouse 31
    'Memorator' 32
    William Devey 34
    W.J. Davis 38
    B.J. Round 41
    C.A. Vince 43
    George Barnett 45
    W.J. Clarke 49
    Sir William Cook 51
    Frank Wright 53
    William McGregor 55
    Simeon Doggett 57
    Sir Francis Lowe 59
    Edward Taylor 61

Illustrations 64
Index 79
About the Author 83

Acknowledgements

This book is dedicated to the memory of the photographic historian Pete James. I knew Pete for over thirty years and outside the central library, inside the central library, on trains, over lunch in pubs and cafes, on Colmore Row, and in many other places, we would discuss my projects and his projects. Our friendship began with our shared interest in the Victorian photographer Sir Benjamin Stone, but I also owe Pete a great debt for the assistance he gave me with other books in this series of Birmingham Biographies. I know that what Pete did for me, he did for many other people. His generosity and support will always be remembered by all those who knew him.

Over the course of putting together this book, I came up with a number of questions to which I was not able to find the answers myself. Fortunately other researchers were able to do so. I wish to thank the following people for answering my queries: Anthony Joseph; Judith Joseph; Caroline Archer-Parre; and Len Smith. I have also profitably discussed aspects of Victorian Birmingham with Ewan Fernie, Andrew Reekes and – over many years – with Roger Ward.

I have been extremely fortunate to teach some fantastic adult education classes at the Birmingham and Midland Institute. I wish to thank all those people who have attended my classes on Victorian Birmingham for their interest, enthusiasm and contributions.

I should record that, in assembling this book, I have made extensive use of the British Newspaper Archive. All of the illustrations are from my own collection, with the exception of the cartoons and photographs from the *Dart* and the *Owl*, which are reprinted by permission of the BMI.

As ever, my thanks to Richard Brown for managing this project.

Preface

Between June 1907 and April 1909 the *Birmingham Gazette and Express* published over a hundred recollections of the events and personalities of Victorian Birmingham. A champion of the Conservative cause, the *Gazette* had been published each morning in the town since May 1862, with its roots lying in the famous weekly newspaper *Aris's Birmingham Gazette,* founded in the mid-eighteenth century.[1] These sort of nostalgic articles were not unusual in the provincial press of the time, but these particular reminiscences – each of about 1,500 words in length - do demonstrate the great civic pride that was felt in Birmingham. Though the tripe restaurants, street fairs and eccentric pedlars were recalled with affection, all of those who contributed were convinced that the town they lived in was vastly improved from the one they had first known in the second quarter of the nineteenth century – in its buildings, in its public works, in its institutions, in its politicians, in the habits of its people. So Henry Hack recalled in great detail his part in improving the gas supply to the town, Alfred Dickinson remembered how he was employed to introduce electric tramways into the town, J.T. Middlemore described the emigration schemes to Canada he organised for poor children and Edward Townsend wrote proudly about the expansion of the Deaf and Dumb Institute in Edgbaston during his twenty six years as headmaster.[2] These writers were not just recalling what had happened over the previous century, they were offering an interpretation that most its inhabitants would have endorsed – that the spirit of progress had transformed Birmingham.

---

[1] Over the decades the newspaper made adjustments to its title. When it was launched in 1862 as the *Birmingham Daily Gazette,* it was in the hands of men known for their Tory opinions, amongst them Sampson Lloyd, J. Satchell Hopkins and Edward Gem (whose father had had a significant stake in *Aris' Gazette*). The *Birmingham Daily Post,* 27 September 1870, tartly observed that 'if we may judge from the prohibition against transfer of shares to women, married or single, it will not be an advocate for advanced women's rights.'

[2] See *Birmingham Daily Gazette,* 15 June, 22 June 1907, 3 July, 31 July 1908. J.T. Middlemore was a surgeon and Liberal Unionist MP for North Birmingham from 1899 to 1918. The Deaf and Dumb Institute was a longstanding Birmingham institution, opened as far back as 1814.

These recollections offer an illuminating portrayal of Birmingham's nineteenth century. They provide us with eyewitness accounts of a range of events, some of them momentous such as the great Newhall Hill meeting of May 1832 and the Bull Ring riots of June and July 1839. They also add colour and detail to our understanding of what was happening in the town. Who would have thought that the town known for its brass bedsteads, buttons and glass also produced a prize-winning strawberry? Who knew that the resemblance of the radical agitator George Edmonds to a frog was a subject for discussion for Brums? Who was aware that the leading Tory Richard Spooner, wounded at being described as the ugliest man in Birmingham, set out to find a man uglier than himself?

We learn in these stories about matters that are now difficult to discover much about – such as cock-staking or dog fighting and other cruel sports or what it was like to attend the private schools which operated across the town for the sons of the middle class. The political and religious leaders of Victorian Birmingham left deep impressions on these writers. There is not a bad word said about John Bright and Joseph Chamberlain. We get close to understanding the depth of admiration for Bright – he might only have visited the town once or twice a year, but he was venerated for his sincere commitment to democratic progress set out, in each visit, in thrilling speeches in the town hall. And Chamberlain was seen as a doer, a man of action not a man of talk. However, these articles also suggest that we need to make adjustments to how we see some aspects of Victorian Birmingham. It is quite clear from these accounts that the button manufacturer John Skirrow Wright has been completely overshadowed by Bright and Chamberlain and has not received his historical due. From the 1850s onwards this formidable political organiser and campaigner was a key figure in reform politics in the town and, as much as any man, the creator of Birmingham Liberalism.[3] Similarly, our writers rescue from unmerited obscurity John Casebow Barrett of St. Mary's Church,

---

[3] See S. Roberts, 'John Skirrow Wright: The Benefactor whose Statue was Destroyed', in *Birmingham Historian,* 33 (2008), pp. 11-15. I now think this article should have stated more emphatically Skirrow Wright's importance in the establishing Liberal dominance in Birmingham.

unquestionably the most popular and talented Anglican preacher in the town.

Unsurprisingly all the contributors were male, financially comfortable and looking back on successful lives – as manufacturers or solicitors or architects. The only working man to contribute was W.J. Davis, but, as secretary of the Amalgamated Society of Brassworkers, he earned a salary which enabled him to live a different life to his members. Recollections like these need to be treated with caution – events can be inaccurately remembered or re-interpreted. In fact, careful checking has shown that in these accounts there is a remarkably high degree of factual accuracy. Undoubtedly, however, there has been re-interpretation – John Deeley, for example, tells the classic Victorian story of how his application and determination enabled him to rise smoothly from lowly origins to a position of wealth and respectability.

The hundred or so articles published in the *Gazette* in 1907-9 offer us first-hand accounts of Victorian Birmingham. The contributors write of events which they themselves witnessed or participated in. In this sense, there is a real genuineness about them. These stories are undoubtedly an important historical source. I have selected twenty five of them and, in doing so, tried to encompass as many topics as possible – the physical appearance of the town, the arrival of the railways, leisure, law and order, manufacturing, religion and politics. I have shortened each of the pieces and, in terms of content, placed them in roughly chronological order. I hope this collection will encourage others to delve into these fascinating glimpses into Birmingham's nineteenth century.

Recollections of Victorian Birmingham

Charles Lee [1]

I remember the great reform meeting on Newhall Hill, which took place in 1832.[2] I was about nine years of age at the time, but my boyish memories of the mighty demonstration are as fresh as in my youth and indeed seem ineffaceable. My father took me to the meeting, which was naturally an attraction to sightseers as well as ardent reformers. On that day the shops and factories were nearly all closed, the bells were clanging from church steeples, flags were flying from the windows and mottoes expressive of the zeal for reform were displayed on every hand. Not from the town alone, but from all the district for miles around, did the people stream up in thousands to the huge sand bank of which Newhall Hill was then composed. Headed by bands and banners, there came miners from the Black Country, silk and ribbon weavers from Coventry, workers from the salt mines at Droitwich – regiments of men in such a host as I have scarcely ever seen since.

Young though I was, I have a distinct recollection of the hush which fell upon the crowd when the 'hymn of liberty' had been sung in unison and a trumpet heralded the speech-making and Thomas Attwood, the famous leader of the Political Union, stepped to the front of the hustings which crowned the hill.[3] Taking off his hat with a reverent gesture, Attwood said, in ringing tones, "Men of Birmingham, I want you all to copy me, to take off your hats and say after me 'God Save the King'". The whole multitude roared the words as one voice – and there was perhaps no more striking

---

[1] Charles Lee (1823-1914) was prominently involved in Freemasonry in Birmingham. This article was published in the *Birmingham Daily Gazette*, 3 April 1908.
[2] The demonstration took place on Monday 7 May 1832 and, according to its organizers, attracted 200,000 people from Birmingham and the surrounding area. With mounted marshals overseeing the arrival and dispersal of the spectators, this important display of support for parliamentary reform was very carefully organized and controlled by the Birmingham Political Union.
[3] 'The Gathering of the Unions' (also known from its first line as 'God is Our Guide') was sung by reformers not only in 1832 but long after. It was attributed to the Birmingham Unitarian minister Hugh Hutton.

testimony to the political power which Attwood wielded at that time. For the loyalty to the throne of those who favoured reform was often questioned, and this was Attwood's method of proclaiming that the men of Birmingham could be sturdy and uncompromising reformers and yet loyal subjects of the Crown.

As a lad in my teens, I saw the riot in the Bull Ring, when the mob burned down a grocer's shop at the corner of Moor Street and the police were despatched from London with orders to break up the Chartists' meetings and arrest the leaders.[4] It was the appearance of the London policemen which greatly added to the resentment of the people, who pulled down the railings of St. Martin's and St. Thomas' churches and used the iron as weapons of defence. The military had to be called out before peace was restored, while many of the townsmen were enrolled as special constables for the protection of property. They numbered two thousand or more and were on duty for certain portions of the day. I have a truncheon which belonged to my uncle. The Birmingham police of that day were few in number: they wore blue coats and red collars and were usually elderly men.

In those days, I remember, the old cock pump stood in the Bull Ring, below the chancel of St. Martin's Church. It was approached from outside, and men used to fill cans of water and retail them to householders at a half penny a pailful. The town was then entirely dependent on its pumps for a water supply, and the cock pump of St. Martin's was the source for Bull Ring people. I remember that when St. Peter's Church was burnt down, water had to be fetched from Digbeth in carts for the purpose of pouring on the flames.[5] The streets were lighted with oil lamps. When the cemetery was being constructed in Warstone Lane, men used to

---

[4] The Bull Ring riots took place over a fortnight between 4 July and 22 July 1839. The peak of the disturbances was on the evening of 15 July when the crowd seized control of the Bull Ring and a grocer's shop and a bedding shop were set alight. See C. Behagg, *Politics and Production in the Early Nineteenth Century*, (1990), pp. 202-22.

[5] St. Peter's Church in Dale End burnt down in January 1831, a few years after its completion; it was immediately rebuilt but demolished at the end of the century. See *Aris's Birmingham Gazette,* 31 January 1831.

wheel barrows of sand from the bank in which the site was being cut out all the way to Lodge Road, their wages being a penny a barrow.[6]

I recall a stormy Easter vestry when there was a scrimmage for the parish books and, when one of the leaders of the row got possession of them, he stood on the books while he harangued his followers. This occurred in '37 at a meeting called to elect the churchwardens of St. Martin's and to make a church rate, which was frequently the subject of unseemly altercations at vestry meetings. On this occasion trouble followed a contention that the rector had no right to act as chairman while the parishioners elected their warden. The parish books were demanded to be shown, and the vestry clerk's refusal led to a pandemonium during which the rector's pew was smashed to pieces and the meeting ended in disorderly brawl.[7]

It was, I think, in 1837 that I saw the first railway train leave Birmingham from Vauxhall and in the following year I saw one start to London for the coronation. The trains came no further into Birmingham than Vauxhall, where the locomotives were uncoupled and the coaches hauled by ropes into Curzon Street station.[8] My first railway journey was an excursion from Birmingham to Gloucester. The third class carriages had no seats and the passengers had to stand, even all the way to London. You were not allowed to take your portmanteau into the truck for fear you should make a seat of it. All the baggage was piled on top of the coaches, a system which often led to mishaps such as trunks being lost on the way or the luggage catching fire.

---

[6] Warstone Lane cemetery, intended for the burial of Anglicans, opened in August 1848.

[7] The leading figures in this protest are not identified here but were the metal manufacturer George Frederick Muntz and the radical speaker George Edmunds. Both were subsequently tried for riotous assembly but acquitted. A detailed report of the event, regularly punctuated with such observations as 'Great uproar, cheering, hissing and hooting', was published in the *Birmingham Journal*, 1 April 1837.

[8] A temporary station was created at Vauxhall until that at Curzon Street was completed. Watched by a crowd of thousands, the first passenger train, consisting of eight first class carriages, set off from Birmingham for Liverpool and Manchester at 7 a.m. on 4 July 1837; a train carrying second class passengers left at 8.30 a.m. See *Birmingham Journal*, 10 July 1837.

'An Octogenarian'[9]

The first event which I recollect outside my father's house was the second of the great meetings on Newhall Hill, in the month of May 1832.[10] There was an agreement come to that every reformer should wear the Political Union badge, which consisted of blue silk ribbon with a union jack in the middle, to be worn on the breast. I was carried to the meeting, my father putting me on his shoulder to survey the assemblage. Memory left on my mind an impression of the very large number of people, with flags and banners, but, as a child, I was naturally much more impressed with the splendour of my badge than with the size of the meeting. The next public demonstration I saw was the chairing of the first two members of Parliament for Birmingham under the Reform Act in December 1832. These were Thomas Attwood and Joshua Scholefield. They had a carriage drawn by six horses, and, with a display of flowers and flags, they went around the principal streets of Birmingham.[11]

When I was about ten years old my parents were desirous that I should go to King Edward's Grammar School in New Street. If there was any preliminary examination I was qualified to pass it, for my father had taught me to read and write and also elements of arithmetic, algebra and geometry. Entrance to the school was, however, then obtainable by nomination by a governor and my parents had no social influence with any of the governors and failed to obtain a nomination. I was sent to a private school. The master was a most beautiful penman, and he received a larger income from copying documents for the attorneys than by teaching. In the morning he would set the boys certain lessons and then quietly get on with his quill-driving till the boys were ready to be examined. The master of my second school was more conscientious, but had never been trained as a teacher and I left school at the age of twelve with little more instruction than I had received from my father.

---

[9] This is an amalgamation of two articles published in the *Birmingham Daily Gazette,* 21 November, 28 December 1907.

[10] The first meeting took place on Monday 3 October 1831, and, according to the BPU, was attended by 150,000 people. Attwood and Edmonds were the main speakers.

[11] Attwood and Scholefield were returned unopposed. Scholefield was de facto deputy of the BPU.

The Mechanics Institute and the Polytechnic Institution had courses of ten or twelve lectures given by George Shaw and Dr Melson, and these I diligently attended.[12] I often got admission to the lectures of the Philosophical Society, which occupied a brick house in Cannon Street. In that house was a most delightful lecture room, which could hold at a pinch about three hundred people, and this afforded me one of the delights of my life. There I had the pleasure of hearing R.W. Emerson deliver two lectures in 1847.[13] I also had the advantage of occasionally listening to literary lectures of a very high order. I especially recollect a course of lectures on Jewish history delivered by the Rev. Dr Raphall, the rabbi of Birmingham synagogue.[14] During the whole of my boyhood and young manhood I derived very great benefit from lectures and, by the time I was twenty one, I do not suppose any young man in Birmingham had heard more lectures than I had.

At one time writing was taught in the Wesleyan Sunday School attached to the Cherry Street chapel and my father, who was a most competent man for the post, was writing master. But I recollect some Sabbatarian superintendent of the circuit denounced the teaching of writing in a Sunday School as being a desecration of the Sabbath and he was successful in excluding writing from the Sunday School. My father was so indignant at this that he resigned his post.

In July 1839 the Chartists held several disorderly meetings in the Bull Ring and, although the magistrates had forbidden them to assemble, they persisted in doing so. A number of London police

---

[12] The Mechanics Institute was formerly opened in March 1826 and put on lectures and also arranged classes in mathematics and drawing. It was funded by a small subscription, paid annually or quarterly. When it closed in 1843, the Polytechnic Institution was created to provide public lectures but became extinct in 1854. George Shaw was responsible for issuing patents in Birmingham and delivered lectures on chemistry, when he styled himself professor. Dr Melson was a surgeon at the Queen's Hospital, Bath Row.

[13] The American essayist Ralph Waldo Emerson arrived in Britain in October 1847 and his lecture tour reached Birmingham at the end of the year. The audiences for his lectures were 'principally composed of the elite of the intellectual aristocracy of the town' but these were some mutterings that he had simply read his lecture on Napoleon. See *Aris's Birmingham Gazette*, 25 December 1847.

[14] Rev. M.J. Raphall served the Hebrew congregation at Singers Hill synagogue and the Hebrew national school from 1841 until 1849, when he left for America. He was noted as a man of considerable learning. I am grateful to Judith Joseph for this information.

were sent for to assist the constables of the town, who comprised a very small and inefficient number of elderly men. There was some mistake in the first instance as to the magistrates authorising the police to act; but on a Monday in July a large body of Chartists armed with clubs came up the Bull Ring and, not being controlled, set fire to two houses – one being that of Thomas Bourne, a grocer – at the corner of Moor Street and the Bull Ring. I recollect seeing Dr Melson, who was a newly-appointed magistrate, riding at the head of a regiment of foot soldiers and a squadron of cavalry to quell the riot. The cavalry tried to use the flats of their swords only, but they had to use more severe measures. When, on the following morning, I went as far as Cherry Street, there was evidence of a severe struggle having taken place between the mob and the soldiery, for blood was to be seen on the doorsteps where one or other had taken shelter.

My father and grandfather took pains that I should grow up to be a zealous Liberal. They took me to the town hall on the occasion of a tea meeting by the Anti-Corn Law League, the reason why a charge was made for the tea and admission being that the Chartists used to disturb the open meetings of the League. On that evening I first saw and heard Cobden and Bright, both excellent speakers but with a different tone. Cobden was a debater, full of lively argument and illustration. Bright was more serious and declamatory. He was clad in the black cloth of a strict member of the Society of Friends. Little did I think that, in after years, I should live to see his black hair turned to silvery white and often meet him at the houses of Charles Sturge and George Dixon.[15] I well recollect his distrust of Palmerston's treatment of all active Liberal principles and his meddling and warlike diplomacy. At a dinner party at George Dixon's just after Palmerston's death in 1865, he expressed his delight that there was now a chance for earnest Liberal legislation in place of the tepid and half-hearted support of Palmerston.

Although not privileged to attend any of the social entertainments of the better classes in Birmingham when in my

---

[15] Charles Sturge was the younger brother of Joseph Sturge and, whilst more active in business, shared his reform credentials, being a member of the town council for forty four years. The two brothers paid the expenses of John Bright when he was returned for Birmingham in 1858. George Dixon was elected to the town council in 1863 and at a by-election four years later joined Bright in representing Birmingham in the House of Commons.

youth, I happened to hear a great deal from the conversations of others who were present at such gatherings. Oyster suppers and whist were diversions for winter evenings. One well-known story of my youth concerned a gentleman who, though an eminent scholar, had not been blessed with physical courage. One evening, at a whist party in Temple Row, he was requested by a lady, who wished to tease him, to take her across to the other side of St. Philip's churchyard, which was not infrequently the resort of bad characters. "Good heavens, madam", exclaimed the unfortunate gentleman, "and, if I do, who will bring me back again".[16]

Edward Preston [17]

Middle class education was chiefly to be obtained in private academies, of which there were several in the town. One of the most noted was Bristow's, a school situated at the corner of the Old Square and the Lower Priory. The Rev. Edward Bristow belonged to the Unitarian body but took no part in the public affairs of the town. A short, stout, florid-haired man was Bristow, a very nice man in his way, save when he lapsed into occasional bursts of temper. He was well-read in a variety of subjects, a master of languages and mathematics and well able to control his school of thirty to forty boys. The school was carried on entirely by himself, and, not only did he look after the boys in daily attendance, but he found time to take extra pupils of a large growth. Frequently during school hours young men would come to him and, sitting at his table, take instruction in Euclid and mathematics. Besides the usual elements of education, Latin, French and other languages were taught at Bristow's school.[18]

The Old Square was really square-like, with massive houses having iron railings in front of them. At the four corners of the

---

[16] Dee's Royal Hotel in Temple Row was the chosen venue for the town's elite for dances and whist parties.

[17] Edward Preston (b. 1835) was a manufacturer of measuring devices and an active supporter of the Unionist cause. This is an amalgamation of two articles published in the *Birmingham Daily Gazette,* 13 November, 28 November 1908.

[18] Preston's father had established the measuring devices business in 1825 and was able to afford the fees of eight guineas a year that Bristow charged; but he kept his son at the school for only a short period and did not avail himself of tuition in Latin and Greek at an additional charge of two guineas.

Square there were stands for four-wheeled cabs – 'cars' we used to call them. The drivers were like a flock of robin redbreasts, with their blue coats set off by red waistcoats. At election times the Old Square was always the location of one of the wooden booths erected for polling purposes. I remember the first parliamentary election taking place in Birmingham. An election usually meant a concourse of drunken people. If one side offered the free and intelligent voter a pint of beer, the other side outbid it with the proposal of a quart!

Prominent among the politicians who figure in my earliest recollections of Birmingham life was George Edmonds, who took a leading part in the local demonstrations in support of the reform movement of 1832. He had a powerful voice and was a forcible speaker; his chief facial characteristic was a large mouth. Whenever he was caricatured in the public prints, Edmonds was usually depicted as a frog on account of his mouth. He was a great agitator, a restless man, always "agin the government" over something or other. The authorities finally stopped his mouth by making him clerk of the peace when Birmingham became incorporated.[19] Then there was Joe Allday, another familiar personality, who lived in Union Street and ultimately rose to the mayoral chair. If anyone asked who and what was Joe Allday, he would be told that Joe kept "a tripe and bird cage establishment". This remarkable admixture of business arose from the simple circumstances that, while he was himself a wire-worker, his wife kept a tripe house. Joe was a Liberal and so fluent of speech that he could talk all night. The little tripe shop in Union Street was quite a centre of political debate. I remember Joe frequently coming to talk with my father, who was continually being asked to enter the town council, though he would never consent.[20]

Those were the great days of the alehouse politician. The Woodman in Easy Row was a noted resort of local politicians,

---

[19] The clerk to the peace was an administrative role providing assistance to the magistrates.

[20] Joseph Allday entered public life in 1828 as the scourge of the local elite who he bitingly attacked in his *Monthly Argus and Public Censor*. Repeatedly sued for libel, he was he imprisoned for bankruptcy. From 1849 until 1859 he was the leading figure amongst the dominant group on the town council known as 'the economists'; but did not, as this writer states, become mayor. See R. Ward 'Joseph Allday: Scapegoat for Municipal Backwardness', *Birmingham Historian*, 32 (2008), pp. 18-23.

especially of the Tory colour. Many were the projects hatched there. In Lichfield Street existed another popular Tory house. This was the Nag's Head, at one time kept by John Westwood, a highly respectable and respected publican, who afterwards become the proprietor of the more famous Woodman. The Liberals also had a house in Lichfield Street - the Old Star, where Whigs and radicals would fraternize.[21]

I recall the time when it was the practice among the poorer classes to fetch the coffins required for the burial of the dead from the workhouse authorities, and I particularly remember the effort of a poor Irish woman to carry home the coffin in which her dead husband was to be laid. The coffin was too weighty for her strength and she struggled along the street till, by way of having a rest, she reared it up against the door of my father's tool shop. The sight of the coffin thus placed on his door step put my father about so much that he protested to friends on the town council and Poor Law Board against the inhuman practice of making the poor carry home their coffins. The protest had the ultimate effect of securing the amendment of the shameful custom and thereafter the coffins were place in the charge of able-bodied men and conveyed in covered handcarts in a more respectable fashion. In those days, too, when a tramp sought a night's lodging at the workhouse, he was inspected through a trap door and told to produce his order. The 'casual' had first to procure a note from some respectable householder or shopkeeper - my father gave many such notes in his time - or without it he had to wait, however wet the weather might be.

Familiar frequenters of the streets of Birmingham were various peculiar personages. There was Jimmy the Rockman, whom I can remember from the time I was about five years old. Jimmy was an old army pensioner who used to parade the streets in breeches and leggings and a green coat. He carried in his hand a tin can full of sticks of rock or toffee, which Jimmy sold as a specific for coughs and colds. It was amusing to hear his cry of "Cough! Cold! Cough! Cold!", as he shuffled along with his can full of rock.[22] Another 'peculiar' was Jim Crow, who sang and danced wherever he went.

---

[21] In May 1860 John Woodward acquired the Woodman from his brother-in-law James Onions; and Edward Sprawson and Alfred Heaton, respectively, took over the Nag's Head and the Old Star.
[22] Jimmy the Rockman's real name was James Guidney; he died in September 1866, aged 84.

There was also a third Jimmy – Jimmy the Whistler, who had a face like a parrot and could whistle like a bird.

Among other peculiar habitues of the streets were the tumblers. These tumblers would go around in troupes of four at a time. Their performance consisted of turning somersaults and various other acrobatic feats, for the execution of which they carefully spread a carpet. The Old Square was a noted pitch for the tumblers. There were not many open spaces, except the actual streets, for casual performances of this description and most of the streets were narrow and ill-paved.

I also have a recollection of the London policemen coming down to Birmingham to assist in quelling the great riots which accompanied the Chartist agitations. At the time there was no regular police force in Birmingham - the town only had men called Runners. The appearance of the London policemen created no little sensation. They were dressed in blue tail coats, adorned with brass buttons and in white trousers, this uniform being crowned by shiny top hats.

Alfred Davenport[23]

Birmingham, in the days of my earliest remembrance, was policed by ten men, who wore surtouts closely buttoned up, with red collars and top hats and they were always called 'red-collar men'. They were usually recruited from among the prize-fighters, who were numerous enough in Birmingham in those days. Perhaps the most noted of these policemen was Billy Hall, who was also an ex-prize fighter. Hall was very much feared and hated in the town.[24]

At night the town was protected by about twenty or thirty old soldiers, who were called 'Charleys'. They wore no uniform but dressed in overcoats and carried policemen's lanterns and also sticks in their hands and handcuffs in their pockets. During the night they called the hours and state of the weather, and in return received from each householder a penny or two pence a week,

---

[23] This article was published in the *Birmingham Daily Gazette*, 16 January 1908.
[24] *Birmingham Daily Gazette,* 15 November 1869: 'I remember the time when Billy Hall, with his ash plant, would clear a whole street single-handed of disturbers of the peace, for, with all Billy's faults, he was a resolute officer and a terror to evil doers'. William Hall held the post of superintendent of police from 1842 until 1845.

which they used to collect from house to house on Sunday mornings. This was the only remuneration they received, as the authorities paid nothing.

Each 'Charley' had a watchman's box. These boxes had doors which opened outwards, and they were usually placed just on the causeway at a street corner and, when the night was wet and snowy or when 'Charley' felt like having a nap, he would retire within his box. It became a sportive diversion for the young bloods of the town, when returning from a dinner or dance, to run the box against the street and place it against a wall, or to overturn it in such a manner as to make the door impossible to open from within so that the luckless 'Charley' was imprisoned in his own box till help arrived.

When the Birmingham police force was reorganised, Billy Hall became chief and, after this, he began to feel his feet too much. Indeed he would be quite rude to the magistrates and ultimately his incivility and arrogant audacity earned his dismissal. Hall next kept a public house in Worcester Street, and sank lower still in later years. The last I saw of him was when he used to sit at the top of a flight of stairs in the Quadrant, gathering a scanty dependence from charity.

Prize-fighting and dog fighting were the two principal amusements among the working classes.[25] It was the practice to train men for the ring in connection with certain public houses, the licensees of which would offer prize money and thereby attract to their custom men who sought the acquaintance of the champions of the prize-ring and of all its following. The fights invariably took place in some rural spot on the outskirts of the town. One noted prize-fighter was known as 'Solid'. When he gave up the ring, he took to a public house in Tower Street. That was the one ambition in life of these prize-fighters – to win a few combats and, with the prize money, to take a public house. Dog-fighting was very popular and a favourite resort for a Sunday morning bout was in the vicinity of the river Rea. Another thing for which Birmingham used to be noted was its bad money. Wherever you went elsewhere in the

---

[25] The police sought to intervene in prize fights and dog fights. Prize fighters were bound over to keep the peace on a surety of £25 and the men who organized dog fights were each fined five pounds; if these financial penalties could not be met, they were sent to prison. See *Birmingham Daily Post,* 16 September 1863, 29 April 1865, *Birmingham Journal,* 16 December 1865.

country, people who discovered that you came from Birmingham would bite your money suspiciously.

John Deeley[26]

My first year's work was with my father in the steel toy polishing trade. The premises were part of Muntz's metal-rolling mills in Water Street, and I remember Muntz well. He was a big, broad, bearded man who invariably carried a walking stick. He was one of the first Members of Parliament for Birmingham. At that time nearly all the ingot metal made in Birmingham was cast at this mill, for the lighting of which Muntz made his own gas.[27] My first situation really was at Wallbank & Bassett's, who had a metal concern in James Street, near St. Paul's Square.[28] I remember how proud I was to take home the first half a crown I earned. I was a caster's boy and it was the practice at that time for the boys to go to work before the men so that they might get things ready and set the pots. I used to trudge through the streets of Birmingham at four and five o'clock in the morning on my way to work. The metal ingots were cast at this place and, as casters were often sent out to different places where regular casters could not be kept in constant employment, I had to go out with these men. So I went to Clifford's mills in Fazeley Street, to John Aston's in St. Paul's Square, to Finnemore's and several other factories.[29] This continued from the time I was nine till I was thirteen, when I

---

[26] John Deeley (b. 1825-1913) was the owner of the gun makers Westley Richards. Whilst his wife and daughter ran a boot and shoe shop he rented, he worked as a clerk for the steel toy maker James Heely and, in 1860, joined Westley Richards. His elevation was the result of the patents he secured for improving the mechanism of guns. For many years treasurer of George Dawson's Church of the Saviour, he was an active Liberal. He was known for his passion for bowls. This article was published in the *Birmingham Daily Gazette,* 29 June 1907.

[27] G. F. Muntz became extremely wealthy as the result of his invention of 'Muntz metal' – on which he took out patents – which was used in the manufacture of bolts and shearing for ships. He was one of the founders of the BPU and, from 1840 until his death, one of the town's MPs. There is an entry for him in the *Oxford Dictionary for National Biography.*

[28] Charles Wallbank and Thomas Bassett were brassfounders.

[29] John Aston was a button manufacturer and leading Birmingham Tory. Joseph Finnemore was a pen manufacturer.

became very unwell. The sulphur used to get on to my chest and I was advised to give up this work. Before I was thirteen, however, my employers were giving me nine shillings a week. I went to the office of a Leek silk manufacturer, Benjamin Fanshaw Heywood by name. I went there as an errand boy, and, in the last five years I spent in Mr Heywood's employment, I managed the Birmingham branch myself. Part of my duties was to go round to the tailors and drapers of Birmingham to solicit orders.

Starting to work at the age of eight meant that I had little or no schooling and my only chance to be educated was found in attendance at Sunday Schools and night schools. So I went to a school connected with St. George's Church in Tower Street. John Garbutt was the rector and he was a great reader. It was an excellently conducted school and a feature was the holding of instruction classes. One of these was conducted by the late Dr. Prince Lee, headmaster of King Edward's School. A fine man was Prince Lee. He gave us lessons in anatomy one evening a week, and, to illustrate his lessons the better, he brought a splendid skeleton.[30] Then there was a very good library associated with the school and of this I made very full use. I devoured biography, history and philosophy. I instructed myself in grammar and arithmetic. I had all the grammars that were published I should think. Next I made up my mind to master the French language. My working hours were long, however; I was frequently late at night and never sure of getting away in good time and so I used to knock up my French teacher at seven o'clock in the morning. My French stood me in very good stead in after life. For instance, when in the employ of Henry Edwards, a general merchant in High Street, I undertook all the correspondence that was necessary in the French language.[31]

My arithmetic proved useful, too. Lomas Harrison, the accountant, asked me to enter his offices in Waterloo Street. My accountancy work did not end with my engagement under Lomas Harrison for, when I went to Westley Richards, to whom I was recommended by my old employer, Henry Edwards, I found no

---

[30] James Prince Lee was chief master of King Edward's School in New Street from 1838 until 1848. He left to become the first Bishop of Manchester.

[31] Henry Edwards was a jeweller, silversmith and cutler. He was often away from Birmingham, attending to his business interests in London.

balance sheet had been made up for three years. With the aid of the stock books and other ledgers and with knowledge I had now obtained as an accountant, I was able to make up the three years' balance sheets satisfactorily. From that time I applied myself to the gun trade in which I have led a busy life ever since.[32]

John Suffield [33]

Of Queen Victoria's coronation day in summer 1838, I have a distinct recollection. It was a very fine, warm day, and the whole town was given up to public rejoicing. The bells of St. Martin's were ringing with such vigour as to rock the steeple, and this gave the first warning of the unsteadiness of that structure. Indeed bell-ringing was for the future only practised in a very gingerly fashion, and some seven or eight years later a fund was raised by public subscription for the rebuilding of the spire. Subscriptions flowed in from all classes and creeds, my father, who was numbered among the Carr's Lane congregation under Angell James, subscribing cheerfully to the fund.[34] I was christened at St. Philip's Church on the same day as the Prince of Wales was baptised. The occasion was honoured as a national holiday, and places of business in Birmingham and elsewhere were closed. By this time I was eight years old and therefore remember the cross of water on my brow very well.[35]

---

[32] William Westley Richards founded this famous manufacturer of military and sporting guns in 1812.

[33] John Suffield (1833-1930) was a shopkeeper in Bull Street. He sold shirts, collars, gloves and similar items. His business lasted from 1829 until 1884 when he ran into financial difficulties. He was the grandfather of J.R.R. Tolkein. This article was published in the *Birmingham Daily Gazette*, 10 April 1908.

[34] John Angell James (1785-1859) became pastor of Carr's Lane chapel in 1805 and was joined by R.W. Dale as co-pastor in 1854. He drew large congregations and some parents named their children after him. On the fiftieth anniversary of his appointment, he was presented with a cheque from his congregation for £500 - to which he added another £500 of his own money to provide financial assistance to aged and impoverished clergymen. He wrote extensively, notably the widely-circulating *Anxious Enquirer* (1834) and *An Earnest Ministry* (1847). He was buried, amidst very emotional scenes, underneath his own pulpit, but disinterred and reburied at Witton cemetery in 1970. Obit. *Birmingham Journal*, 8 October 1859.

[35] Albert Edward, later Edward VII, was christened at St. George's Chapel, Windsor, on 25 January 1842. It was good news for the six hundred inmates of

I remember the comings of Queen Victoria to open Aston Park and of the Duke of Cambridge to open Calthorpe Park.[36] An incident of the Duke's visit is noteworthy. George Reeves presented his Royal Highness with a very handsome sword, and, in doing so, conveyed a hope that the Duke would do something to retain this manufacture in the country. The Duke took the remark as a personal solicitation for orders and was very indignant; he gave the sword to the superintendent of police before he left Birmingham. Queen Victoria's visit was naturally an occasion of great local jubilation. If anyone happens still to possess one of Breese's photographs taken at the moment the Queen was entering the town hall, they will see the royal foot peeping from beneath the royal petticoats. Charles Stanton Breese was the originator of instantaneous photography and for many years was an artist employed at Peyton & Harlow's bedstead factory and engaged in decorating paper-mache.[37] When the Queen reached Aston Park, she was received with eloquent emptiness all the way from the gates up to the hall for, although two miles of seats had been provided on each side, there were at that spot few spectators since the high prices charged for these seats deterred would-be occupants and this part of the arrangements proved a fiasco for the Aston Hall Company.

I saw the great Jenny Lind on one of her visits to the town, and, not only saw and heard her, but even sang on the same concert platform. I was a young chorister at that time, and, together with a number of others, received lessons in the Hullah method from a music master named Elliott and we were giving an exhibition of singing at the town hall on the same night that Jenny Lind was the

---

the workhouse in Birmingham who were provided with a roast beef dinner; the elite attended a ball at the town hall. See *Aris's Birmingham Gazette,* 31 January 1842.

[36] The visit of Queen Victoria on 15 June 1858 was the first visit by a reigning monarch to Birmingham. For a full account see C. Chinn *Free Parks for the People*, (2012), pp. 46-50. Also ibid., pp. 33-36 for the visit of the Duke of Cambridge on 1 June 1857. A cousin of Victoria, he was commander of the British army. The newspaper reports of the day do not mention the sword he handed back.

[37] Charles Stanton Breese produced stereographs, described as 'the most popular form of photography throughout the mid-nineteenth century before Eastman's Kodak popularized small snapshots' (*Times Literary Supplement,* 13 April 2018; letter from I. Christie). He earned his living by decorating the top-of-the-range beds of Peyton & Harlow which were priced at one hundred guineas.

star.[38] At later dates I have recollections of the visits of Moody and Sankey, the famous American evangelists. Such a stir did they cause that their midday meetings in the town hall were crowded to suffocation and they were obliged to take Bingley Hall for the big meetings.[39] And what a sea of mud there was all the way up Broad Street. Rowley rag was used in those days for street paving because it was a pleasant surface in fine weather. In wet weather, however, it cut up into deep mud, which in Broad Street would often rise above one's ankle.[40]

Always a great centre of religious life, Birmingham has been stirred in the past by many notable preachers, of whom I have some recollection. At Carr's Lane in my young days, there was John Angell James, whose kindly, beaming face redeemed it from entire ugliness. Though not a learned man – he was only a promoted draper's assistant – Angell James would as a preacher often rise to great heights of eloquence and he certainly commanded a huge following. His *Anxious Enquirer* was said to have sold at one time in greater numbers than even the New Testament. As a man he was good but narrow, and against tobacco he had an inveterate enmity. In the pulpit he would declare, "I tremble for the salvation of any young man whom I see with a cigar in his mouth." He would denounce Byron freely as a poet "unfit to be touched." He greatly vexed and mortally offended Sam Timmins by preaching at him at his father's funeral. Poor Timmins never forgave him.[41] Other popular preachers of those days numbered J. Casebow Barrett of St. Mary's – a bachelor who used to receive many pairs of slippers from his feminine admirers and a most eloquent man – R.A.

---

[38] The Swedish opera singer Johanna Maria Lind enjoyed considerable success in Europe and America. Her earliest appearances in Birmingham were at the town hall in August 1847 and August 1848. George W. Elliott taught the pianoforte and organ and singing according to a method popularised by John Hullah. He secured patrons by styling himself a professor of singing.

[39] Ira Moody preached and Dwight Sankey sang at these events. For a report of one of their packed meetings in the town hall see *Birmingham Daily Post,* 23 January 1875.

[40] Rowley rag was a stone quarried in the Black Country.

[41] Sam Timmins was a hardware manufacturer and bibliophile and closely associated with George Dawson and Joseph Chamberlain.

Vaughan, the saintly young preacher at Ebenezer Chapel, and, of course, the inimitable George Dawson.[42]

'An Old Architect'[43]

My earliest recollection of Birmingham is of the great disappointment and vexation I felt on hearing that the man to whom I had been articled in London, where I had fulfilled three of the six years of my apprenticeship, had decided to remove to Birmingham, and the annoyance of my friends who had not foreseen and guarded against such a contingency in my articles. When my chums heard of the coming transference, I was much chaffed at the prospect of becoming a 'Brummagem Button' and, in reply to a feebly expressed assertion that Birmingham was an important and even celebrated place, they unanimously agreed that it was chiefly famed for the excellence and large consumption of tripe. Now it curiously happened that as I was passing away from Curzon Street station by way of some recently cut street for conveniently approaching it, I saw fixed to the back of one of the adjacent houses a rough board rudely inscribed with the words 'tripe and cow heel'.

I found my way into High Street and called at a hatter's shop kept by J. Gittins - I remember his name because I always got my hats from him from that time forth - and inquired how best to get to the Bristol Road. Whilst waiting in the shop, I watched him serve his customers and was amused at seeing him try customers' hats on his own head to judge the required size. I was very kindly directed by him and, just as I was leaving the shop, was startled by the noise of the town crier's bell, followed by an announcement that 'tripe and cow heel of an excellent quality will be read at Joseph Avery's at seven o' clock'. A few days after, one of my first acquaintances in Birmingham took me to a tripe supper at the Bull's Head in the Minories, where I was initiated into the mysteries

---

[42] John Casebow Barrett was the incumbent of St. Mary's for forty three years. His obit. describes him as being 'for some years ... the most popular preacher in Birmingham' (*Birmingham Daily Post,* 28 February 1881); Robert Alfred Vaughan (1823-1857) was the incumbent of Ebenezer Chapel in Steelhouse Lane from 1850 until 1857; ill health compelled him to resign and he died in London.

[43] This article was written by 'a veteran and widely-known architect' and published in the *Birmingham Daily Gazette,* 10 January 1908.

of 'heels' and 'shoes' and other analogous delicacies. I was much interested in the old-world aspect of the room in which they were served. It was large but low-ceilinged, with bare boarded floor, fireplace wide, with a high chimney shelf on which were iron racks of long clay pipes and a brass tobacco-box, pipe lights and a few candlesticks. A number of small round deal tables, Windsor chairs and triangular spittoons completed the furniture of the room. Beer was served in old-fashioned stoneware jugs and drunk from tall slender glasses. The atmosphere was laden with the 'mild mellow' odour so much approved by Trotty Veck and about a dozen elderly men were either feeding or smoking.[44] They were, I afterwards found out, wealthy and important personages of the town. I was very pleased with the place and my supper.

I was entertained temporarily at the house of a well-known townsman in the Bristol Road, near the bottom of Priory Road, where there stood an old toll house gate. Piggott Smith reconstructed the road from this point to Springfield Street. The road was straightened, guttered and kerbed and soon after the lime trees for which a subscription was raised from the inhabitants were planted.[45] Some few refused to subscribe and, to mark these, some young men went round late at night and whitewashed the trees opposite their gates. I remember a solicitor called Dick Underhill, who lived near the bottom of Sir Harry's Road. He took great interest in the local improvements and, I believe, originated the idea of planting trees in the Bristol – certainly Sir Harry's – Road. He was an amateur fruit grower of local repute and a large but rather coarse and poorly-flavoured strawberry was produced by him and called the 'Sir Harry'.[46]

I think it was in 1849, the year in which I came to Birmingham, that I was standing in the Bull Ring whilst a peal was rung in St. Martin's tower and was amazed by the extent to which the spire rocked, so much so that it seemed as if the weathercock must be jerked off. Having very good eyes I noted, too, that the stonework near the summit was much decayed and the mortar gone

---

[44] Trotty Veck, an impecunious, aged messenger, is the main character in Charles Dickens' *The Chimes*, (1844).
[45] Piggott Smith was employed by the street commissioners as their surveyor.
[46] Richard Underhill was a town councillor for Edgbaston. His strawberry won many prizes; twenty plants could be obtained from him for one pound and he also wrote a manual on the cultivation of strawberries.

from the joints. On returning home, I described what I had seen to my principal, who went to look at the spire and who wrote a letter to the newspaper, urging the necessity of an immediate inspection and that the ringing of peals should be stopped until that had been done.[47] Mr Hardwick, an architect from London, was then called in and laddering was erected to the top. I was one of the first of those who ascended the weathercock. Mr Hardwick was employed by the London and North-Western Railway, to build the offices to New Street station and the finely-proportioned front to Stephenson Place was designed by him.[48]

Shortly after my arrival in Birmingham I went with some others to Drayton Manor to see the funeral of Sir Robert Peel. The party, of which I was the youngest and most insignificant member, comprised some interesting Birmingham men. I remember Samuel Lines, the artist, Daniel Hill, the architect, and, I think, Peter Hollins, F.W. Fiddian and others.[49] The weather turned out wet, and altogether the excursion was disappointing. The present Sir Robert had been hastily called home from Switzerland and he attracted a good deal of attention.

In my early days I was very fond of the theatre, and I well remember most of the members of the stock company of the Royal. The Gardeners, father and daughter, were there. The company included that extremely funny low comedian, Bobby Atkins, who made me laugh, I think, more than any other comic actor I have seen. On every occasion of a performance there was an interval for a dance by Monsieur and Mademoiselle Gilmer. Holder's in Dale End was a great success, very much frequented and very soon enlarged and remodelled. Day's Concert Hall in Smallbrook Street was originally but a small public house, taken by a barber James Day, whose old shop and pole I well remember. Day converted the little inn to a gin shop and, to create an attraction, purchased some

---

[47] See *Aris's Birmingham Gazette,* 18 February, 17 June 1850.
[48] Philip Hardwick also designed the now-demolished arch at Euston station.
[49] The funeral of Sir Robert Peel took place on 9 July 1850. Samuel Lines was one of the founders of the School of Art and the Society of Artists in Birmingham. He painted landscapes and taught drawing to many local artists. There is an entry for him in the *Oxford Dictionary of National Biography.* Peter Hollins was a sculptor with a studio in Great Hampton Street. He produced work for Bodelwyddan Castle, amongst other places. Daniel Hollins and F.W. Fiddian were architects.

articles that were sold at the dispersal of the Great Exhibition, the chief of which was a gigantic glass mirror and a great silver globe of glass pendent from the ceiling. These proved great attractions and the country people came in large numbers to see them.[50]

There were but two or three places in town where one could get a decently served lunch or dinner other than the inns and hotels. I took my modest meal for some years at Bensons, but occasionally at Mrs Meek's in Church Street and later at Nock's in Union Passage.[51] There was a little room at the back of Bryant's confectionary shop at the corner of Congreve Street which a few prominent men of the town used to frequent, George Dawson among them. Good substantial dinners were provided at the Gough Arms by St. Martin's Church, the Acorn in Temple Street and the Coach and Horses in Congreve Street.

Bingley House and Baskerville's house were still standing. I went to the former just before its demolition and measured its fine Georgian staircase with a view to re-erecting it in a house built for the Rev. R. Evans, rector of St. George's Church, Llandudno, where it still exists. A little incident relating to the last days of Baskerville's house may be worth recording. Whilst the workmen were making the preliminary arrangements for pulling it down, Samuel Timmins and I met by appointment at the house and walked through the rooms of each floor, from which the boards were just being stripped. It occurred to each of us that it might just be possible some of Baskerville's celebrated type had fallen into some of the joints of the floor or other crevices and we searched anxiously but in vain.[52]

---

[50] *Birmingham Journal,* 18 February 1854 for an advertisement for 'this gorgeous establishment, already the wonder of everyone …'

[51] *Birmingham Daily Post,* 21 December 1859: 'For comfort and economy, dine at Nock's, 13 Union Passage, Birmingham. Soups, fish, game, poultry and hot joints from twelve till four. Fresh joints daily at two o'clock'. John Nock was the proprietor.

[52] Bingley House was owned by the banker Charles Lloyd; in March 1850 it was dismantled and its marble chimney pieces, staircase, doors, floor boards, bricks etc sold off. John Baskerville's house passed in 1817 into the hands of Benjamin Cooke who incorporated it into new buildings for the manufacture of rods. The house was abandoned in 1880 and demolished in 1888. I am grateful to Caroline Archer-Parre for this information.

William Downing[53]

I well remember the appearance of New Street when at the top end there stood the old fire engine in a shed-like structure. The town had limited provision against fire in those days, and this was one of only two engines. Sometime later the fire engine station gave place to a house of much resort when Joe Hillman left the Acorn Hotel to establish his own snack bar, the first of the kind in the town. Across the way, at corner of Ann Street, stood Bryant's, the pastry cook's, practically the only confectioner's establishment in the town worthy of the name. For those of us who were young fellows in those days, however, Bryant's was a place of luxury for the charges were scarcely moderate. Behind the shop was a little back room where teas were provided. The room would scarcely hold ten people. Here a cup of tea and a slice of bread and butter, so thin and wafer-like that a breath of wind would blow it off the plate, would be retailed at seven pence while a small glass of milk cost two pence.

From Ann Street an omnibus started for Handsworth every twenty minutes. It was a big, lumbering vehicle, drawn by three or four horses and often containing only as many passengers and it was one of the spectacles of the day to watch the bus start away. From the High Street end of New Street another omnibus, single-horsed, started for Five Ways every half hour. Traffic generally in the streets of Birmingham was then of an exceedingly meagre description.

Fair week was one of the great events of the town, and I have seen the streets from Smithfield to St. Martin's crowded with stalls laden with gingerbreads, sweet stuffs and fancy articles. An open space was largely taken up by penny shows of all descriptions, comprising the usual fat woman, the dwarf, the giant and all the rest. There was a theatre, too, somewhat larger than a booth, a skeleton structure of wood with a tarpaulin roof, and here performances were given at frequent intervals. We could see 'Othello' and 'Macbeth', and an amount of drama, compressed into ten or fifteen minutes performance and charged at the rate of two pence to the pit and a penny to the gallery. The bill of the play at Fair time was full of 'blood and thunder', desperate murders and the thrilling rescues

---

[53] This article was published in the *Birmingham Daily Gazette*, 5 December 1908.

of virtuous females. The amusing thing was that often the people outside had as much entertainment as those who had paid their pence to go inside. The clown - there was invariably a harlequinade following the heavy pieces - in all his motley would pirouette along the street, accompanied by an elegant young lady scantily dressed in the guise of Columbine.[54] Nor was this all the entertainment obtainable. Paget's show was an attractive and at one time regular feature. It was pitched in Dale End and usually filled the space, even across the carriage way. At the bottom of Martineau Street there would be Wombwell's menagerie. It was a big affair and different prices were charged for the morning, afternoon and evening shows.[55]

Above all there was a procession in which the firemen and many of the principal townsmen took part, and in which a conspicuous figure was the town crier, clad in gorgeous raiment. I remember old John Wilson, the bellman or public crier, very well. He wore a cocked hat and carried a large bell, which he rang as he gave out announcements on things lost and found, of forthcoming events, and other matters of public concern. A curious character was Gutteridge, the 'currency man'. He was, I remember, a man of large proportions and he usually wore a heavy overcoat in which were capacious pockets. These pockets were always stuffed with handbills relating to the currency question, on which, according to Gutteridge, depended the whole salvation of the country.[56]

Close to the terminus of the Handsworth omnibus in Ann Street was the office of a famous lawyer in the town, George Jabet by name. Besides being a sound man of law, held in much-respect by his fellow townsmen, Jabet was a man of letters and a leading light in local literary circles. He wrote under the pseudonym of Eden Warwick, publishing *Notes on Noses* and *The Poet's Pleausance*. An interesting personality was George Jabet.[57] Another

---

[54] Columbine is a character from open air comedy associated with Italy.

[55] See *Aris's Birmingham Gazette,* 5 June 1854, for details of the performing elephants, the only travelling rhinoceros in the country, the lions and tigers and other animals that Wombwell's toured around the towns of England. Admission cost 1s with an additional 6d in the evening to witness feeding time. George Wombwell died in 1850 and the business was taken over by James Edmonds.

[56] The subject of a paper currency greatly interested the Birmingham reformers.

[57] George Jabet was a Tory but had close relations with George Dawson and his circle through his love for Shakespeare's works and involvement in the

noteworthy figure was a publican named Westwood, who at one time kept a small public house in Lichfield Street. Westwood was a well-read man, very much liked by all who came in contact with him, a man of very gentlemanly appearance and of large culture, who in all respects might be said to be superior to his calling. When he left Lichfield Street, he took the Woodman in Easy Row, that famous hostelry which played so large a part in the shaping of the public affairs of the town in those days. Westwood adorned the place with literary portraits and encouraged discussion on literary and public affairs so that the Woodman became the favourite resort not only of town councillors but of many leading tradesmen, merchants and professional men.

One of the most remarkable personages of the day was the Rev. Casebow Barrett, the eloquent and popular vicar of St. Mary's Church in Whittall Street. It was a veritable treat to hear Casebow Barrett read the lessons – so admirable was his elocution. He was in his day the fashionable preacher, and all the fashionable folks of Birmingham crowded to his church. Unless one went to the service very early it was impossible to enter the church, still less to secure a seat. Barrett himself had a curious individuality. He had about him all the characteristics of a dandy. He was always faultlessly dressed; there was nothing soiled or frayed about him; he wore stays that kept him trim of figure and affected an elegant scent which scattered its perfume all about him. But with all his dandified style Casebook Barrett was a man of acknowledged ability. He was a man of marked literary tastes and at the vicarage he had a library well stocked with books. In the pulpit he was an eloquent and forceful preacher who exerted an undoubted power and influence over his congregations.

Of Elihu Burritt, who became the first American consul in Birmingham, I have distinct recollections as a man remarkable for his perfect simplicity, whether of dress or demeanour. No one outwardly regarding him would imagine him to be the notable man he was. Elihu Burritt, who knew sixteen languages, was a great reader, and he would frequently come into the old Chaucer's Head

---

subscription and the public libraries in the town. *Notes on Noses* (1852) was a humorous attempt to classify people according to their noses; the *Poet's Pleasaunce* (1847) was an anthology of poetic quotations. Obit. *Birmingham Daily Post,* 15 July 1873.

in New Street and there wait for the bus which would take him home after the official labours of the day. The bus stopped almost at the very door, but it would invariably come too soon for Burritt, who would stay to discourse among the books.[58]

T.H. Aston[59]

My father, John Aston, was a great friend of the vicar of St. Peter's, and held the office of churchwarden for several years. I well remember the two going arm-in-arm to the great town hall meeting which was held in the year of the 'Papal Aggression', 1850.[60] Speaking of the town hall, at that period of controversy and resistance, the Maynooth question being then carried on with great heat, I will relate that my first recollections of town hall meetings was of the one held in 1853 when the members of the Birmingham Protestant Association presented the member for North Warwickshire with a splendidly-bound Bible for his long-continued services in resisting the payment of an annual grant to the Roman Catholic college at Maynooth.[61] Richard Spooner was a grave speaker and spoke in solemn tones and with intense earnestness of purpose. He was everywhere spoken of as 'Maynooth Spooner'. He was a banker, not very handsome in features, and a story is told that he undertook to find an uglier man than himself but, according to the narrator, Dickie Spooner failed in the attempt.

Although young, I was a frequent purchaser of tracts at the shop of Thomas Ragg, a bookseller who occupied premises at 90 High Street. Ragg edited and published the *Protestant Watchman* of Birmingham and the neighbourhood. He was, I understand, in

---

[58] Elihu Burritt was an American peace campaigner who felt he fitted in well with the progressive culture of Birmingham, where he formed strong friendships. He was United States consul in the town from 1865-69. A great walker, he wrote several books about his perambulations.
[59] T.H. Aston was secretary of the Protestant Association in the town for almost half a century. This is an amalgamation of two articles published in the *Birmingham Daily Gazette,* 5 March 1909, 10 April 1909.
[60] See *Aris's Birmingham Gazette,* 16 December 1850. 'Papal aggression' was a term coined to describe the creation of Catholic dioceses across England.
[61] See *Birmingham Journal,* 9 July 1853. In accepting his Bible, Spooner vowed that 'he would never cease in his endeavours until this Protestant country discouraged, by every means in its power, the propagation of such doctrines as were taught at Maynooth.'

the forties editor of the *Birmingham Advertiser,* and a man of considerable literary capacity. Subsequently he was the author of a book of great value to Christian apologists, this being *Creation's Testimony to its God.* I remember and value his friendship. He was my hero of those days; I emulated his courageous Christian advocacy and his influence on myself cannot be forgotten. How much could I tell about Thomas Ragg, and of his ordination being offered him by a bishop and accepted without university preparation! It was my privilege to arrange two nights' debate at the Temperance Hall between the newly-ordained townsman and George Jacob Holyoake.

In 1860 I was elected secretary to the Protestant Association. The bringing out of a daily Conservative newspaper inspired me with hope for the cause in which I was engaged and I frequently obtained insertions of my correspondence.[62] Father Sherlock and a Roman Catholic police inspector – I think his name was Kelly – were very bitter against my work. While William Murphy was holding his service in a wooden structure in Carr's Lane a crowd assembled outside my father's premises on the afternoon of Sunday, June 16, and smashed all the windows.[63]

There was a large number of Irish residents in London Prentice Street and the neighbouring outlets and also in Park Street. When disturbances were threatened the mayor George Dixon became timid and the authorities nervous to a degree. Having consented to arrange a course of lectures in Birmingham by William Murphy, I was appealed to not to proceed. I applied for several of our public buildings but only to find that police notices had been served and they were not to be obtained for lectures by Murphy. The town hall was refused by George Dixon and, notwithstanding a requisition to him signed by 2000 persons, he stoutly refused to sanction the delivery of the lectures and went so far as to say that Murphy should not lecture in Birmingham. We had a stiff fight for supremacy and a wooden structure was constructed on some vacant land in Carr's Lane adjoining the chapel. There was much excitement in the town during the

---

[62] See, for example, *Birmingham Daily Gazette,* 23 April, 18 May, 7 September 1863.
[63] Thomas Cairo was convicted of this offence and bound over; John Aston secured compensation.

erection of this temporary building. The Roman Catholics became defiant and the feebleness of the mayor, together with the inaction of the chief of police and the watch committee, brought about the disgraceful disturbances which ensued. Columns could be filled with the details of that eventful visit when Liberalism was completely dominant and yet freedom of speech was denied to those who did not bow the knee to Caucus dictation. We fought for freedom of speech and the Liberal dictators found their tyrannical sway was quickly disappearing.[64]

F.W. Humphreys[65]

One of my earliest musical memories relates to the first performance of 'Elijah' in Birmingham town hall. I was a boy-chorister in that famous festival and, during the interval, some of us found our way to a room beneath the platform set apart for the principals. In this room stood a grand piano which, happening to be open, looked so inviting that I was tempted to strum a few chords. In a moment there came up to me - who but Mendelssohn himself! "Ah", said the great composer, seating himself on the music stool, "you should play so" - and he imitated my stiff, straight fingers - "but you play so". And, for a few delightful moments, he played as only Mendelssohn could play. Then he patted me on the head and exclaimed again with a kindly smile, "you should play so".[66]

Alfred Mellon recommended me to Mercer Simpson and, in 1858, I was appointed director of the orchestra at the Theatre Royal - a post which I held for forty two years.[67] As I first remember the

---

[64] William Murphy was an anti-Catholic lecturer of great notoriety. His name was given to the violent confrontations between his supporters and Irish Catholics in Birmingham in June 1867 which saw great destruction of property. For a useful discussion of these events see J. Moran, *Irish Birmingham* (Liverpool, 2010), pp. 62-88.
[65] F.W. Humphreys (1834-1909) conducted the orchestra at the Theatre Royal. He had been a chorister in the production of Mendelssohn's 'Elijah' at the town hall in 1846. He died after falling down the stairs at his home. This article was published in the *Birmingham Daily Gazette*, 4 January 1908.
[66] See A. Duggan, *A Sense of Occasion: Mendelssohn in Birmingham, 1846 & 1847* (Studley, 2011).
[67] Alfred Mellon was director of the Royal Italian Opera at Covent Garden. A Birmingham-born violinist, he had been bandmaster at the Theatre Royal.

New Street playhouse, there were no stalls and the pit extended round the orchestra to the stage. The frequenters of the gallery were keen critics in their way. It was no uncommon occurrence for a bit of touching pathos on stage to be spoilt by the noisy descent of a bottle from the top tier. It was quite a popular amusement to drop a bottle on to the big drum and not infrequently the drumstick operator went home on a Saturday night with well-developed bruises all over his cranium.

The first pantomime with which I was associated at the Theatre Royal was a production of 'Red Riding Hood'. The stage manager was Bobby Atkins, a well-known personality. The operatic ballads of Balfe and Wallace were frequently introduced into the pantomimes and a popular ditty sacred to the clown was 'hot codlings'. Nowhere more than at the Theatre Royal was the music hall element longer resisted and repressed, for Mercer Simpson was a stickler for the older traditions. A succession of artistes who subsequently made big names in the theatrical or variety worlds made their early appearances on the boards of the Theatre Royal. Somewhere in the early eighties there was Vesta Tilley coming on as Prince Charming in 'Beauty and the Beast' and one can recall the enthusiasm she evoked with 'Oh, you girls' and 'The March winds do blow.' There was Harry Randall, too, with his 'Ghost of Benjamin Binns'.[68]

In those old days Shakespearean drama was played more frequently than now. Not always with financial success, however. I remember Tom King, popular tragedian though he was, playing Shakespeare to an almost empty auditorium while a circus up the street was drawing crowded houses. "You don't seem to pull them in, Tom", remarked a candid friend as he peeped at the beggarly array of empty benches from behind the circle. With a sonorous groan, T.C. King responded, "How can a poor tragedian pull against seven elephants?"[69]

Mercer Hampson Simpson was manager of the Theatre Royal from 1864 until 1891. He succeeded his father, who took up the post in 1837. In his younger years Simpson was an accomplished boxer, rower and fencer. See obit. in *Birmingham Daily Gazette,* 14 August 1902.

[68] The stage names of, respectively, Matilda Powles and Thomas Randall. Both enjoyed lengthy pantomime careers at the Theatre Royal.

[69] Thomas Charles King, noted for his deep voice, often played Hamlet.

Samuel Edmonds[70]

Most of my early memories are centred in the gatherings of which the Hope and Anchor was the scene. In the fifties there were no large assembly rooms available for club meetings and the like and the Navigation Street house was the favoured resort not only of numerous sick societies and money clubs, but also of important political meetings.[71] There was a large room in which popular concerts were held on Saturday and Monday evenings and some of the finest singers brought to Birmingham appeared on these occasions - Rigby, Bickley, Forman among them. No females were allowed to be present and everything was conducted in a quiet and orderly fashion. On one occasion, I recall, there was a farewell concert given by a band of the Scots Greys just before they left to go to the Crimea and the band of another regiment stationed in Birmingham gave another concert.

But the Hope and Anchor was popularly associated chiefly with the famous series of Sunday debates. This debating society, which was conducted on strictly parliamentary lines, was a school of education in political and social questions such as existed probably nowhere else. It arose in the fifties just about the time of the Crimean War and began with the reading and discussing of the news from the front and it went on for thirty two years. Every Sunday night there were crowds in Navigation Street waiting in rows to get into the house. The debates were continued all the year round in, on winter nights and in summer evenings alike, and the interest in them was maintained in wonderful fashion. The first 'speaker' or chairman was Samuel Morton, who was a delineator or surgical artist, and the vice-chair was usually filled by my father, Robert Edmonds, or Bob as he was familiarly known to all the town. The father of this debating society was a well-known Liberal named Dorman. Other leading debaters whom I remember as among the best orators of these Navigation Street meetings were Jeremiah Thom, who was a prominent Forester, Allen Dalzell,

---

[70] This article was published in the *Birmingham Daily Gazette,* 8 May 1908.
[71] Meetings to organise municipal election campaigns were regularly held at the Hope and Anchor. During their dispute with the watch committee over improved pay in autumn 1859, the police constables of the town made use of it for meetings.

George Bill, Charles Hibbs and Joseph Lampard, who was, at one time, a member of the town council.[72]

Often times were parsons and teetotallers to be numbered in the gathering, debating social problems. It was at one of these Sunday night meetings that the project was first mooted of organising a reform demonstration, the outcome of which was the memorable Brookfields assemblage of 1866.[73] As the political house of that day, the Hope and Anchor became the resort of rival politicians of rising eminence and its speakers included at various times G.F. Muntz, J. Skirrow Wright, George Dixon and John Bright. One of the Sunday debates was opened by Henry Broadhurst, and other Members of Parliament met friends and foes and discussed the measures of the day in that upper room in Navigation Street.[74] We were careful to admit only respectable persons who could be trusted to take an intelligent interest in the proceedings and to create no disturbance, however heated the arguments might become. Neither was any approach to drunkenness allowed at any time. All unsuspected, the company included one night the notorious Irishmen, Daly and Egan, who were subsequently convicted of complicity in the dynamite plots. No doubt they were attracted by a prospect of the Irish question coming up for discussion.[75]

It was in the forties, and by friends of my father who were frequenters of the Hope and Anchor, that the Artisans' Penny Fund was started, with Alderman Palmer as chairman. A tablet which was placed in the vestibule of the Queen's Hospital in 1847 records that

---

[72] All of these working men politicians have left traces of their activities in support of reform causes behind in the Birmingham newspapers. The former Chartist Allen Dalzell was described as 'the greatest blackguard in the borough' (*Birmingham Daily Post,* 14 May 1858).

[73] The demonstration took place on 22 August 1866 with up to 200,000 people in attendance. See S. Roberts, *The Chartist Prisoners: The Radical Lives of Thomas Cooper (1805-1892) and Arthur O'Neill (1819-1896),* (Oxford, 2008), p. 134-5

[74] Henry Broadhurst was Lib-Lab MP for Bordesley in 1885-6.

[75] John Daly and James Egan were residents of Birmingham and in August 1884 were convicted of planning to throw grenades into the chamber of the House of Commons. It was soon claimed, however, that the explosives had been planted on Daly. See M. C. Frank, *The Cultural Imaginary of Terrorism in Public Discourse,* (2017), pp. 100-2.

a sum of £985 1s 3d was paid to the Hospital Fund.[76] While this collection was going on, I remember that a deputation, including my father, waited upon the Rev. Dr Miller, rector of St. Martin's, in connection with business pertaining to this Artisans' Fund and it was suggested that it would be a good thing to have a collection for the local hospitals made simultaneously in all the places of worship in the town on an appointed Sunday. This idea was taken up by Dr Miller and J.S. Wright, who was at the time editor of the *Midland Counties Herald,* with results to be seen in the great success of Hospital Sunday collections in latter days.[77]

I remember signing on for the Volunteers at Whateley's office in Waterloo Street, and in the course of a few years became a sergeant in the company commanded by Captain Harry Gem.[78] We had several bothers about the question of uniform. Particularly I do remember a grey uniform with which we were provided. It was a nasty, uncomfortable sort of dress, completed with a cap in which was suspended a big, drooping feather. It was through my Volunteer associations that the Hope and Anchor became a regimental as well as a political resort and the scene of numerous Volunteer dinners. One of the most notable of these was a gathering which was by way of a send-off to the Garibaldi Volunteers. Forty young men of Birmingham had volunteered for service under the famous Italian patriot, and they proceeded to Italy under the leadership of a young fellow of the name of Porter. When in 1886 the Midland Railway Company bought the house and pulled it down for important extensions, Navigation Street lost a familiar feature and Birmingham orators and patriots a favourite haunt.

---

[76] See *Birmingham Journal,* 4 December 1847. John Palmer was mayor in 1854-5.
[77] Rev. J.C. Miller was rector of St. Martin's from 1846 until 1866. Obit. *Birmingham Daily Post,* 13 July 1880.
[78] Whateley's was the most prestigious firm of solicitors in Birmingham. John Welchman Whateley succeeded his father and his clients included the Calthorpe family, King's Edward's School and the Great Western railway. A Tory, he lived at Edgbaston Hall. Obit. *Birmingham Daily Post,* 10 December 1874.

Henry Moorhouse[79]

Habits of life in Birmingham, such as I remember to be familiar features in the fifties and early sixties, have in many respects undergone a complete metamorphosis. There was a time within my own recollection when every street had its own baker, who was usually very busy on Sundays cooking dinners for almost all dwellers in the street; when every street had its boot and shoemaker; and it was quite common to meet the brewer who brewed for four or five public houses in the vicinity or the pig killer, with apparatus on his back. Shrove Tuesday was a notable day in town for it was a custom among publicans to boil peas and bacon in large quantities in the brewing furnaces and to serve out a jorum of this delectable dish to any customer who cared to call with a basin or can. Feasting on peas and bacon was usually followed by the boisterous humours of 'heaving day' when the men used to 'heave' the women and kiss them, the ladies having their turn at the game, too. This curious old custom has long died out in Birmingham.

The ordinary sports of the townsmen, the working classes in particular, consisted of pigeon flying, dog fighting, rat pits and cock staking. Pigeon flying was very exciting in its way; the religious element at one time tried to put down this amusement but without avail. A flying match would be arranged, the money put down, and on the Sunday a little crowd would make off into the country with their baskets of pigeons. Dog fights frequently took place in public houses, the largest room being set aside for the purpose, and fairly high prices charged for admission. White bull terriers were mainly used, for these are the most pugnacious fighters of all the canine species, especially if they have been trained for fighting purposes.

Cock-staking, which was quite a different affair to the older pursuit of cock-fighting, was a very cruel sport. A game cock was taken to the chosen ground and tethered by its leg. The sportsman stood at a distance of thirty five yards and, when facing the bird, shot at it. To ensure the cock was facing the shooters it was the practice to bring up another cock in a basket, and the moment the one bird saw the other it would crow. The tethered cock would turn to see where the crowing came from and bang would go the guns. Often times as many as ten or a dozen shots were fired

---

[79] This article was published in the *Birmingham Daily Gazette,* 9 October 1908.

without the cock being hurt, unless some stray shot broke its leg. The bird's breast acted as a shield and to kill the cock at one shot was not so easy a matter. This sport of cock-staking attracted hundreds of people at a time, and a favourite locality for a staking was the Knob. This was a walk across the fields at the far end of Coventry Road, sometimes called Chain Templefields. It was at the Knob that the last cock-staking took place so far as my recollection goes. The sport was put down about 1865 and dropped into total oblivion. The rat pit was another cruel diversion of the period. In pits or cages fifty rats would be loosed at a time – and then the dog would be dropped amongst them. Often the dog would be badly bitten; the victory went to the dog that killed the greatest number of rodents within so many minutes.

Pony racing was another popular sport with Birmingham people. There were races at Deritend Pool three or four times a year, and, following the decline of cock-staking, races were also held frequently on the Coventry Road hill. Another local event was the Sparkbrook Races, held on the Stratford Road. The ponies were specially trained for racing and were often very fleet of foot.

'Memorator'[80]

There must be few now remaining who remember in any detail the appearance of the western end of Birmingham in the earlier half of last century, when Banker Lloyd was still living at Bingley House and the fine trees which grew in the park-like demesne overhung the walls. Five Ways was quite the uttermost part of the urban area. There was a big glass factory whose "cones" used to belch forth great clouds of dense black smoke.[81] A few houses were dotted on either side of the Hagley Road, but there were no street lamps and on the left-handed side ran an open ditch, which was as often as not filled with dirty water and over which brick archways gave access to the houses. The Plough and Harrow was quite an old-fashioned hostelry and beyond this point there lay a stretch of open country, the only exceptions being a few dwellings of red brick on the right

---

[80] This article was published in the *Birmingham Daily Gazette,* 29 January 1909.
[81] The Islington Glass Works of Rice Harris. See S. Roberts, *Joseph Gillott and Four Other Birmingham Manufacturers 1784-1892,* (Birmingham, 2016), pp. 38-48

hand side and Hazelwood House, where Rowland Hill's father had kept a school.[82]

In Ladywood, there were only a few solidly-built mansions, most of which were surrounded by extensive and well-planted mansions. Hereabouts stood the homes of R.W. Winfield, the founder of an historic Birmingham business, of William Chance and of John Unett.[83] On the southern side of Birmingham, suburbia began and ended at Camp Hill, where there were numerous houses built by business men who, in the fifties and sixties, were slowly learning the pleasure and value of retreating from a health point of view from town environments at the end of the day's work. Stratford Road was more or less a country highway, with the Mermaid a welcome house of call.

St. Martin's and St. Philip's were the principal edifices, but the little church of St. Mary in Whittall Street was perhaps the most notable, owing to the highly successful ministrations of the Rev. Casebow Barrett, a popular clergyman. Mr Barrett had come from Hull several years previously and he soon awakened a neglected parish. Before his time it was said that St. Mary's was usually empty at the Sunday services, but Mr Barrett, with his earnestness and eloquence, contrived to effect a remarkable change of things and St. Mary's presently boasted larger congregations in proportion to its limited capacity than any other church in the town. The Rev. Casebow Barrett had an excellent voice and a pale, thoughtful countenance, which lighted up with animation as he warmed to the subject of his discourse. He had, by the way, a certain peculiarity of pronunciation by which his 'u's' invariably sounded as 'a's'. But this did not detract from the effectiveness of his delivery nor impair the forcefulness of his pulpit appeals, and everybody who remembers Mr Barrett will retain an impression of his striking ability. He held the living for many years and became the doyen of Birmingham parsons.

Foremost among Nonconformist divines in those earlier days were John Angell James and Timothy East. Angell James had originally been destined for a commercial career and was

---

[82] Thomas Wright Hill, an advocate of progressive education, founded a boys' school called Hill Top. It was succeeded by Hazelwood School, run by his sons, Matthew and Rowland (later the founder of the penny post).

[83] For Winfield see Roberts, *Joseph Gillott*, pp. 21-37. The brothers William and Robert Lucas Chance were glass manufacturers in Spon Lane, Smethwick.

apprenticed to a draper. But the pulpit was obviously his place in the world and into the pulpit he went at quite an early age. He was an exceedingly popular preacher and drew large congregations to Carr's Lane by his vigorous personality. He had a powerful voice and could at times rise to considerable eloquence. The Rev. Timothy East, who was the well-known pastor of the Ebenezer Chapel in Steelhouse Lane, was equally eloquent and possessed perhaps a greater degree of culture. He was earnest, lucid and logical in his discourses. But then he could write as well as orate and his pen was frequently employed in the compilation of thoughtful and able essays on evangelical subjects.[84]

Among the Roman Catholics the Rev. Father Sherlock was a popular priest who, himself a typical Irishman, speedily won the regard of the large Irish community in the Moor Street quarter of the town. When he came to Birmingham, the mission of which he took charge had no better home than an old workshop in the neighbourhood of Allison Street. Father Sherlock, who was a very tall and well-built man, used to say that he had only five pounds when he came to Birmingham and he did not know what it was to have such money again until long after his people made a presentation to him. He was a powerful factor for peace when the memorable Murphy riots broke out, for he had an influence that weighed with the fiery-tempered fellows of the Irish quarter far more than the whole force of constabulary. It only wanted a glimpse of his stalwart figure to disperse a group of excited Irishmen waiting to catch any Murphyites who might happen to be about. If the Irish men failed to move off, Father Sherlock would go up to them and say "You'd better go home now bhoys and behave yourselves."

William Devey[85]

I well remember all the principal incidents of the campaign in the Crimea, and all the excitement which was occasioned here at home. News came through very slowly and was gleaned from the medium of *Aris's Gazette* and the *Journal,* which were weekly publications

---

[84] Timothy East resigned as pastor of the Ebenezer Chapel in 1843. He protested loudly about church rates and the corn laws. He published religiously-inspired stories and his sermons.

[85] This article was published in the *Birmingham Daily Gazette,* 19 June 1908.

and cost five pence each. As it was not everybody who could afford to buy a paper, it was a frequent incident for a crowd of fifty persons or more to congregate in the streets and hearken to the news read by one of their number. It was about the time of the Crimean War that I first became acquainted with John Skirrow Wright through my attending the Sunday School at the People's Chapel in Great King Street.[86] It was there that I imbibed my earliest political views and formed those opinions which have made me a staunch adherent of Liberalism. I remember getting inside the town hall on the occasion of the nominations when John Bright fought his first election in Birmingham; such a scene of bubbling excitement was never to be forgotten. Even as a voteless youth, I was an eager partisan, with 'Vote for John Bright' stuck in my hat band.

A branch of the Reform League was founded in Birmingham, and I became one of its first members. The great event of this agitation was the demonstration at Brookfields in 1867.[87] I should estimate there were fully 150,000 persons participating in the demonstration, which was proceeded by a monster procession. We marched with bands playing and banners flying. It was estimated that the procession was a mile in length, and it certainly represented practically the whole life of Birmingham, political, trading and industrial. At the general election that followed the candidates were John Bright, George Dixon and Philip Henry Muntz on the Liberal side – Birmingham had three seats in Parliament - and Sampson Lloyd and Sebastian Evans on the Tory side. Both of the latter were pre-eminent men in their own way, Lloyd being a great banker and a sterling man in himself and Evans being a man of high literary attainments and much learning and accomplishment.[88] The three-cornered constituency presented some difficulty to the party organisers till William Harris devised the voting scheme which

---

[86] The People's Chapel was established in early 1848 as the result of an acrimonious secession from Arthur O'Neill's Zion Particular Baptist Chapel. There was no minister, Wright often leading proceedings; the Sunday evening congregation numbered about fifty.

[87] The demonstration took place on 22 April 1867. See S. Roberts, *The Chartist Prisoners*, pp.133-4.

[88] *Birmingham Daily Gazette,* 18 September 1908, for a recollection by Joseph Mullins: 'Mr Evans held the degree of LL.D and those academic letters were translated by his opponents as "Lloyd's Little Dog". At the time of the nominations some rough fellow in the crowd held aloft a pup which was greeted by the surging throng as "Lloyd's Little Dog"'.

became famous as the 'vote as you're told' method. The scheme answered admirably and Birmingham sent three Liberal representatives to Parliament.[89]

I remember Gladstone's first public visit to Birmingham and his speech in Bingley Hall - the greatest of all indoor meetings the town has probably known. Henry Fowler had to propose a resolution. I recollect being impressed by his commanding figure and stentorian voice, which was distinctly heard all over the hall.[90] Gladstone was all movement, all animation, and it was singularly fascinating to listen to him. The enthusiasm which his visit created was remarkable, even for Liberal Birmingham: New Street station was surrounded by thousands, and thousands more followed the statesman's carriage through the streets. Perhaps the best speech which Gladstone delivered here was one in Bristol Street board school, when he became so oblivious to all else but his subject, and so impassioned in his torrential eloquence, that, as he swayed forward, his hand swept his silk hat from the little table on which he had placed it and sent it flying yards away.

Somewhere around 1865 there was founded a society for the study of literature and this afterwards developed into St. George's Mutual Improvement Society. Great interest was taken in politics, while a night school, Sunday services and recreation evenings were among the incidental activities of the organisation in which J.S. Wright, George Dixon, P.H. Muntz, Councillors Morley and James Taylor prominently showed their interest.[91] The Society, of which I was an early member, began to concern itself with local representation on the town council, and the movement assumed

---

[89] Dixon 15,098; Muntz 14,614; Bright 14,601; Lloyd 8,700; Evans 7,061. Philip Henry Muntz was the younger brother of George Muntz. William Harris was an architect and surveyor and secretary of the Birmingham Liberal Association. His 'voting scheme' ensured that votes were evenly distributed between the three Liberal candidates. See A. Reekes, *The Birmingham Political Machine. Winning Elections for Joseph Chamberlain*, (Alcester, 2018), pp. 17-18.

[90] The inaugural meeting of the National Liberal Federation was held at Bingley Hall on 31 May 1877 with Gladstone as the main speaker. A solicitor from Wolverhampton, Henry Fowler was elected an MP for this town in 1880.

[91] H. Morley was a councillor for Duddeston and James Taylor was a councillor for St. George's. Previously Taylor had been secretary of the Birmingham Freehold Land Society, founded in 1847. This organisation sought to secure freehold properties for its members. Obit. *Birmingham Daily Post,* 21 July 1887.

such a measure of influence that no one could enter the council chamber through Hampton ward or St. George's or St. Stephen's without having the Mutual Improvement Society behind him.

The first election on which this influence was successfully exerted was that in which James Whateley was returned in opposition to Thomas Nash. The contest was exceptionally vigorous and exciting. We had a vigilance committee of voluntary workers and this committee discovered that bills and posters of our party were being systematically covered up by the bill stickers of the opposition. The committee resolved to retaliate and for this purpose enrolled a voluntary bill-posting brigade. Cans and brushes were bought for our use, and we made our own paste, and thus equipped the brigade set forth at two o' clock in the morning and proceeded to cover up our opponents' election bills. A friend of mine who was a 'Nashite' lived in Wellington Street, where his enthusiasm had led him to plaster the front of his dwelling with placards which I determined to cover. Mounting a ladder, in the darkness of the night, I plied my brush with zeal if not dexterity, when my friend, hearing a noise, threw up his window to see what was the matter. Instantly I thrust my paste brush into his face and disappeared nimbly down my ladder – and he has never found out to this day who was responsible for the outrage![92] We persuaded William Cook to join the council. I was one of the deputation which waited on him in the first instance, and I remember how he hesitated as to whether he was fitted for the work. However, we prevailed on him to accept nomination. It was the best testimony to the efficiency and devotion of William Cook as a ward representative that from that first election he was never opposed.

It was on the topic of education that I first heard Joseph Chamberlain speak in the Public Office. He was a diffident speaker at that time and frequently lost the thread of his subject. When the franchise was extended, working class voters did not immediately apprehend their powers. One day when canvassing, I called at a house in Staniforth Street, where lived a man who possessed the vote for the first time in his life and who obviously anxious to use it. But his wife declared with some asperity that she

---

[92] See S. Roberts, *James Whateley and the Survival of Chartism* (Birmingham, 2018), p. 21.

would see he didn't give his vote to anybody: "He's only just got it and he shan't give it away as soon as he gets it."

Recalling the political memories of the past, I think a word is due in tribute to the labours of John Skirrow Wright, who was really the forerunner who made the way possible for Chamberlain to effect those sweeping changes in civic administration which have made Birmingham widely renowned as a progressive municipality. I wish to express my deep veneration for J.S. Wright for, of all the public men I have known, none entered public life with a purer purpose, a deeper devotion and energy than did he. His one end was to lift up the people to higher standard of life, political, moral and spiritual, and he was absolutely without personal ambition.

W.J. Davis[93]

I can go back in memory to the Crimean War and the visit which the Duke of Cambridge paid to Birmingham in order to open Calthorpe Park. I was a very small boy at the time, but I have a recollection of mingling with the crowds of spectators, of hearing the salute of artillery fired off and of seeing bulrushes growing in the river Rea. Among my earliest political memories is one of accompanying my father to hear John Bright speak when he and Acland were seeking the suffrages of Birmingham's electors. The meeting was held at Beardsworth's Repository and, even at that youthful age, I noted that John Bright had to suck an orange to lubricate his throat.[94]

Early in the sixties I was employed by Timothy Smith & Sons, who had a large and important brass foundry in New Bartholomew Street. It was not uncommon for the boys to stay late on Saturday nights playing pitch and toss, sometimes till ten and eleven o'clock, because the journeymen were in town hard by, busy 'getting

---

[93] William John Davis (1848-1934) was secretary of the Amalgamated Society of Brass Workers. A man of great drive, he oversaw a considerable expansion in membership. He was elected, with Liberal support, to the school board and the town council. This article was published in the *Birmingham Daily Gazette,* 17 August 1907.
[94] A Peelite Tory, Thomas Dyke Acland came forward in the guise of a Liberal in Birmingham in April 1859. Scholefield 4,282; Bright 4,424; Acland 1,544. Beardsworth's Repository was a large indoor space normally used for the auctioning of horses.

change', as they would say; and we used to have our wages paid to us in the public house. I have known lads to lose all their wages before they had received them. Buttons would be used as counters till the wages were obtained with which to liquidate debts. Years after I helped Henry Broadhurst to secure the passing of the Act which prevented the payment of wages in public houses.[95]

When elected general secretary to the Birmingham Brass Workers' Society in 1872, I was only twenty four years of age and, in the work with which I have now been so long associated, it has been a great advantage to have worked at such firms as Timothy Smith & Sons, Smith & Chamberlain, Strouds, Winfields, Oslers, the Mint, Charles Ratcliff and Joseph Ratcliff.[96] The membership of the Society grew rapidly. Although without capital, we obtained for the workers an advance of wages by way of a bonus of fifteen percent. The brass workers being numerically the largest organisation in Birmingham some life was now given to trade politics and, in 1874, we formed a Labour Association, having for its object direct labour representation, irrespective of the two political parties. I was chosen as chairman of the Association and its first achievement in the direction of achieving direct labour representation on public bodies was the election of myself as a member of the Birmingham school board in 1876 – the first trades union secretary to be elected to such a body.[97] In December 1879 I became a candidate for the town council and was elected. It was prophesised that the Labour movement would destroy the pretty idea of selecting the fittest men and would demoralise to a great extent the representative character of our institutions.[98]

When I went on to the school board there was a practice of summoning men and women who had to explain the non-attendance of their children at school to appear in the daytime,

---

[95] Pitch and toss is a game involving the throwing – and winning - of coins.
[96] All brass founders, turning out beds, chandeliers, gas fittings etc, with the exception of Oslers, who were glass manufacturers, and the Mint, a private operation owned by Ralph Heaton, which produced bronze and copper coins for use in Britain and overseas.
[97] See *Birmingham Daily Post*, 19 October, 28 November 1876. There were soon strains between Davis and the chairman of the Birmingham Liberal Association Skirrow Wright.
[98] See ibid., 2 January, 9 January 1880. Davis was returned unopposed for Nechells.

thereby losing time at their employment. At my suggestion, the board, though with reluctance, established evening sittings of the appeal committee. I also went in for an increase in wages to the workers under the board – the visiting officers and caretakers and this effort met with success. In the town council we had a memorable fight over the reduced wages paid to the scavengers and stone-breakers. I had the co-operation of Conservatives as well as Liberals in an agitation that was protracted over a month and which ended in the public works committee refunding the arrears. And when you see a Birmingham street sweeper clad in his overalls today, you may note one of the first municipal institutions to be placed to the credit of Labour representation. For the public works committee went one better than myself and, besides coming to terms on the wages question, equipped the men with overall suits and provided stone-breakers with sheds, in which to break the stones.

In 1883 I was appointed a factory inspector for Sheffield. Before leaving Birmingham I received at a town hall gathering, presided over by George Dixon, an address and a considerable sum of money.[99] In 1889 I was recalled by the brass workers to Birmingham and resigned the factory inspectorship. At the time of my return we had the biggest strike Birmingham has ever known. Almost concurrently with that I was at the head of the bedstead workers' agitation for a 15 percent advance, and meetings in support were held in churches and chapels and halls and theatres and parks. I remember describing at one enthusiastic meeting how we had financial help from all sections of the community and mentioned that even police men had taken off their helmets on top of buses and had made collections – a story that was greeted with the cry "Good old coppers." These movements were successful, the brass workers obtaining the advance they had asked for and the bedstead workers winning, too, as a result of an arbitration in which I conducted the case for the men.[100]

I have been a parliamentary candidate, but I have never felt very anxious to go to Parliament. I have stood the brunt of a contest with Jesse Collings because it was a Birmingham constituency and

---

[99] See ibid., 24 September 1883. Davis was presented with a cheque for £150.
[100] See ibid., 8 February, 21 February, 7 March 1889, 21 February, 7 May, 27 October 1890.

because he had so changed his views. But instead of succeeding, I received a sound thrashing.[101] I should have fought, too, in west Birmingham had the brass workers been united as a protest against the unfair criticisms of labour leaders by Joseph Chamberlain and in order to test the feelings of the working men on the question of fiscal reform.

B.J. Round[102]

I arrived by train at New Street station, then a comparatively new structure. I went to Alderman Manton of Manton & Hopwood and was given an engagement by that firm immediately upon their seeing examples of my work.[103] Having remained with them for six years, I started in business for myself as a gold-cutter in Branston Street, afterwards removing to Northampton Street, and thus came to settle here permanently. To one who recalls Birmingham with all the impressions then freshly made upon the mind of a stranger, as I was in 1858, nothing is more striking than the general alterations in the externals of the town - wide, open streets with wooden pavements instead of narrow, dingy ways paved only with 'petrified kidneys', big, palatial buildings taking the place of insignificant two-storeyed shops and dwellings which lined even the principal thoroughfares.

The municipal government was in the hands of the economists and among the leading men of the town were Allday, Brinsley, Hawkes, Turner and Wright, the accountant.[104] At a later date I remember taking a petition to the town council during the

---

[101] Collings 6,380; Davis 2,658. Davis wanted to talk about higher wages for working people, but his opponents preferred to discuss his salary as a trade union leader of £840 p.a.

[102] This article was published in the *Birmingham Daily Gazette,* 13 March 1908.

[103] Henry Manton's long municipal career began when he was returned for All Saints' ward in 1852. He campaigned for temperance and was not a stranger to controversy. Manton & Hopwood were jewellers in Great Charles Street. Obit. *Birmingham Daily Gazette,* 24 August 1903.

[104] Of these men, Allday, Hawkes and Brinsley were the most noteworthy. Both Henry Hawkes and William Brinsley became thorns in Chamberlain's side. Of Brinsley, it was said he 'is an erratic man truly but then he possesses an amount of energy that attracts attention.' (*Birmingham Daily Gazette,* 11 June 1863). That year his supporters decided that re-election was not reward enough and presented him, amongst other presents, with a gold watch, a gold chain and a diamond ring.

mayoralty of Joseph Chamberlain. The petition was that of the residents of Northampton Street, who wanted a brick instead of a gravelled footpath. I had met Mr Chamberlain one day in the Bull Ring and asked how we should move in the matter and he told me to bring it before the council in that form at a certain date. I remember being greatly impressed by Mr Chamberlain's manifest aptitude for public work and his capacity for leadership.

I well remember the time when elections were carried on in the old style – you recorded your vote in an open booth and, when voters came up in cabs or cars of the unpopular colour, they had a warm reception from the crowd loafing around the booths. One of the notable stations on such occasions was the junction of Livery Street and Constitution Hill. I recollect the first time William Cook was elected to the town council as a representative of St. George's ward. One of his first utterances in the council chamber was a reference to the dirty conditions of certain streets – thus, to my mind, early indicating his great forte lay in the direction of sanitary improvements.

A notable occurrence in the mid-sixties was the failure of Attwood's bank. I well recollect the panic-stricken feeling which pervaded the town on a chilly March day in '65 when the firm of Attwood, Spooner, Marshall and Co. stopped payment. The bank, which stood in New Street, had come to be looked upon as a very safe and sound institution. The liabilities at the time of the failure were over a million sterling, and the stoppage of payment was an exceedingly serious thing for Birmingham business people. Executors and others who had placed money in their trusteeship in Attwood's bank found themselves in a very difficult position. The situation was minimised by the old Joint Stock Bank taking over the assets and providing immediate relief to the customers of Attwood's bank, whose creditors ultimately received a dividend of 11s 3d in the pound.[105]

At that time cheap traffic was entirely in the hands of omnibus proprietors, chief among whom were Tolley and Allsop. Tolley's omnibuses were very large, the largest vehicles of the kind, I think, I have ever seen. They were invariably drawn by four horses and

---

[105] This event inevitably attracted a great deal of coverage in the Birmingham newspapers: see, for example, *Aris's Birmingham Gazette*, 11 March, 25 March 1865; *Birmingham Daily Gazette*, 11 July 1865.

would hold as many as forty passengers, inside and out. Allsop was a post-horse master who ran his omnibuses from High Street to Aston Park and to Nechells, and he used to do very well indeed, particularly on fete days. The service supplied was regular and the fares reasonable, but the starting of the Aston tramways began to interfere with the prosperity of the omnibus service and Allsop's system was bought out by the Birmingham Cab Company. The early tramways also went through many vicissitudes before they were evolved into successful commercial undertakings.

C.A. Vince[106]

I was trained as a little boy to take an interest in political matters. My father was from about the year 1858 until his death in 1874 a leader of political opinion here and one of the most popular of a remarkable group of speakers who trained the men of Birmingham to think liberally.[107] His enjoyment of political work was keen and intense: he was never happier than when addressing an audience of Birmingham artisans. He was born and brought up in Farnham in Surrey. Farnham was also the native place of William Cobbett and my father's schoolmaster was another Cobbett, a nephew of the great demagogue. One of his early recollections was of a holiday given in honour of Cobbett's first election to Parliament. Politically my father remained a hero-worshipper: his hero was John Bright. The faith in which I was nurtured was that Gladstone was all very well, but that the real savour of Liberal doctrines was to be found in the speeches of Bright.

Even as a very small boy I attended many political meetings with my father. I remember especially ward meetings held in the

---

[106] Charles Anthony Vince (1855-1929) was a schoolmaster-turned-political-organiser on behalf of Joseph Chamberlain. His loyalty to Chamberlain was unbreakable and he was secretary of the Birmingham Liberal Unionist Association, the Midlands Liberal Unionist Association and the Tariff Reform League. He was also leader writer for the *Birmingham Daily Post*. See A. Reekes, *The Birmingham Political Machine*, pp. 169-71. This article was published in the *Birmingham Daily Gazette*, 22 August 1907.

[107] Charles Vince was minister of the Mount Zion Baptist chapel in Graham Street from 1852 until his death. He regularly addressed Liberal meetings across the town and was also a leading figure on the school board. Obit: *Birmingham Daily Post*, 23 October 1874. Also see A. Reekes, *The Birmingham Political Machine*, pp. 71-2.

school room in Frederick Street and at the People's Chapel in Great King Street. The Great King after whom I supposed that street to be named was John Skirrow Wright, whose kindness I hold in grateful remembrance. I was often smuggled into the committee room and on to the platform of the town hall by dint of walking so closely behind my father that I escaped notice of the ticket collector. I recall the pride with which for the first time I had the honour of shaking hands with a real Member of Parliament: it was Auberon Herbert.[108] I heard Bright speak, on his return to public life after a long illness, at the first of the great Bingley Hall meetings. I have painful recollections of the terrific crush in the street before the doors were opened.[109]

Another meeting of which I have a vivid recollection was one held at Cave's Repository, at which my father was the chief speaker. At the end of the meeting, when the better known speakers had had their innings, a much younger man moved a vote of thanks. His speech was brief but I thought it very amusing. That was the first time I ever heard Chamberlain. Afterwards he worked closely with his father in the work of the National Education League and the school board. My father did not live to see Chamberlain a Member of Parliament; but I remember his confident prediction that his friend and leader would someday be Prime Minister.

Of the survivors of the old generation of Birmingham politics, I can recall only one – George Edmonds. He was, I believe, the real inspirer so far as Birmingham was concerned of the movement for parliamentary reform which preceded the Act of 1832 and deserved the statue which in fact was given to a man of much inferior calibre – Thomas Attwood. His reward had been the clerkship of peace. I remember him as an old man of venerable appearance worshipping in Graham Street chapel. He had long disused public work and a generation had arisen which did not know him. I went to his funeral at Key Hill cemetery. There was no public fuss; but it was attended by a small crowd of white-haired

---

[108] Auberon Herbert was an MP for Nottingham. A Tory who converted to Liberalism, he was much interested in philosophy and also wrote poetry.
[109] Having secured the services of Bright, the Birmingham Liberals were determined to put on a big display of support for him: Bingley Hall, normally used for such events as the cattle show, was capable of holding 20,000 people whereas the town hall could accommodate no more than 7000.

working men, the survivors of the army that demonstrated on Newhall Hill, who came to take farewell of their old leader.[110]

In the second agitation for parliamentary reform, I remember seeing both the processions to Brookfields. The demonstrators wore a blue ribbon; and Attwood's statue was appropriately dressed with the same. When Attwood and Spooner's bank failed, I remember seeing the same statue covered with mud flung at it by angry depositors.

George Barnett[111]

It was after hearing George Dawson for the first time in Birmingham town hall one night when I was quite a youth that I was induced to go to the Church of the Saviour, and, after hearing the eloquent preacher in his own pulpit, I went every Sunday, and for year after year, even unto the end. I attended the first class day school, when the able Edward Ball was the master; I entered the night school when the genial J.W. Oliver was presiding over it; and, of the Sunday School, I became a member at the time S.J. Baker was the singularly ardent superintendent and when Sarah Crompton, a popular member of the Crompton family and a sister of Susan Dawson, was the head of the girls' Sunday school.[112] A finer band of voluntary teachers could not be found in all the land than those who were carrying on these schools under George Dawson. Indeed a notable feature in the character of that famous preacher was the element of personal magnetism which gathered about him men and women of a high type of character, and numerous were the friendships made and cemented, many the marriages that followed, working for George Dawson in and about the Church of the Saviour.

---

[110] See *Birmingham Journal*, 11 July 1868. The burial service was conducted by Vince's father.

[111] George Barnett (d. 1908) often delivered speeches at meetings of the BLA and the Peace Society. This article was published in the *Birmingham Daily Gazette*, 10 March 1908.

[112] Edward Ball was headmaster of the Church of the Saviour Boy's Day School in Helena Street for seven years until 1867, when he established the Birmingham Middle Class School in Frederick Street. J.W. Oliver had an especial interest in botany and arranged excursions with his pupils to collect plants on Saturday afternoons; Sarah Crompton's developed her own ideas about teaching which won wide local approval.

Looking back to the days when his ministrations were attracting to his Church many of the most notable public men in local life, numerous incidents characteristic of the fearless independence and rugged strength of George Dawson come to mind. He had a way of speaking out his thoughts regardless of circumstances or surroundings, and frequently he would pause in the midst of an eloquent and moving discourse to administer a rebuke of a personal nature in an aside which all could hear. I well remember that, when the Church was becoming increasingly popular till every inch of space was taken up, people sitting in the gallery started a practice of laying their overcoats aside on a ledge which overlooked the floor. To this Dawson took a decided objection, which was no sooner conceived than voiced. "I must ask you to remove those clothes", said Dawson one day in one of his terrible pauses. "This Church is not a clothes line; it is unsightly to see such things; quite out of place; don't let them appear again!" Another practice which he rebuked with a similar bluntness was that of turning round to look at the clock affixed to the front of the gallery. "If you want to know the time", said the preacher sarcastically, "I will tell you." He was very fond of quoting from the Apocrypha, and on one occasion he observed among his congregation a lady well known to him turning over the pages of her Bible in a vain search. In his inimitable manner Dawson paused to remark that it was useless to go on turning leaf after leaf for what he was reading at the moment was not in the Bible!

One Sunday morning while the service was proceeding there entered a lady who was the wife of a prominent town councillor, and who was a regular attendant at the church, but always as unpunctual as she was regular. She had driven up in her carriage, later than usual, and with a great rustle of silks, made her way down the aisle to her seat near the rostrum. Dawson stopped the service, intently gazing at the disturber, and then quietly observed, "When you have done, we will proceed. Who are you to disturb the worship of Almighty God by coming late? When you do so again at least have the decency to remain at the top of the church till a suitable interval occurs." As a rule the preacher was successful in ignoring the people who coughed loudly, but one Sunday, after a thorough break-up of the weather, his crowded church numbered so many involuntary "barkers" that Dawson had to surrender at discretion. "For the first time in my life", he exclaimed "you have the best of me. We will sing a hymn, offer a short prayer and close the service." And to the amusement of his congregation, he sent them summarily home. It was on this very Sunday that three sisters, daughters of a well-known farmer and lay preacher living in the neighbourhood of Studley, set out to walk all the way into Birmingham on purpose to hear Dawson preach. They walked twenty miles without a rest by the way, but heard no sermon after all.

I might relate many anecdotes illustrative of George Dawson's many-sided character. He was never at a loss for a word, for a happy thought, or a witty phrase, or the tactful thing to do. He was once invited to a Jewish wedding, and it happened that he was asked to propose the health of the bride and bride groom. The only Gentile among the gathering, he rose and said, "In the name of the God of Abraham, Isaac and Jacob, I bless ye, my children." Needless to say the effect was electrical.[113] Essentially a man of broad common sense, Dawson looked with little favour on revivalist meetings. He used to say "I need no band, no drum or trumpet" and he would add that the revivalists "mistook perspiration for inspiration". When a lady asked him how it was that he wore a beard when it was not the custom for ministers to do so, Dawson replied, "So that, madam, I may look as much unlike a woman as possible." Going down Newhall Street on his way to conduct an evening service, Dawson saw a ruffianly fellow mistreating a policeman. Being a muscular Christian when the occasion required, the preacher went to the police officer's assistance, handled the troublesome vagabond in dexterous fashion, and helped to march him off, a prisoner, to the police station.

I have alluded to the magnetism of George Dawson's personality, and how it drew to the Church of the Saviour all sorts and conditions of men, including many of the leading spirits in the public life of Birmingham at the time. To enumerate even a tenth-part of George Dawson's congregation would be to cite the best known names in Birmingham, he dominated with such intellectual force. There were Sam Timmins, John Henry Chamberlain, Follett

---

[113] The reason why the effect of this was 'electrical' was that Dawson was invoking the names of the Jewish patriarchs, thereby showing the highest respect to fundamental Jewish beliefs and the centrality of the Old Testament. In blessing the bride and groom as 'my children', he projected deep and genuine respect to the audience. I am grateful to Len Smith for explaining this to me.

Osler, Benjamin Harris, Dr Sebastian Evans, H.W. Tyndall, Sampson Gamgee, Edward Breakspeare, William Gilliver, T.H. Ryland, R. Peyton, Andrew Deakin, John Lewis, James Hinks, Arthur Ryland, William Brinsley, among others too numerous to mention.[114] The singers in his choir included almost equally well-known townspeople and the congregation generally were active workers in all movements for the public good. I remember being one of the deputation that included G.J. Johnson, Dr Lawson Tait, John S. Manton and William Glydon appointed to wait upon Dawson in the vestry one day to urge him to give up some of his lecturing work and spare his health.[115] But George Dawson was not to be turned from what he considered to be a path of usefulness by any personal consideration. He replied that, if the choice lay between lecturing and preaching, he would give up the preaching for the lecturing he regarded as a mental recreation. He held the conviction that lectures did much to liberalise quiet country towns and out of the way places such as he often visited. Moreover, preaching involved, he said, much preparation. "Do you think", he added in his homely fashion as he stood beside the blazing fire of his vestry, "I can preach to you fellows after all these years unless I specially prepare?" And we had to leave the matter in his hands.

Curious indeed was the extent of George Dawson's influence over varied types of mind. William Rignold, the eminent actor, whenever in or near Birmingham, made a point of attending the Church of the Saviour and he used to declare Dawson the greatest elocutionist he had ever heard. Lawson Tait once told me that Dawson was the only minister who had ever influenced him; and

---

[114] J.H. Chamberlain was an architect, often employed by the town council; Follett Osler was a manufacturer of glass chandeliers and tableware; Sebastian Evans was editor of the *Birmingham Daily Gazette,* a poet and local champion of the Tory cause; H.W. Tyndall was a solicitor; Joseph Sampson Gamgee was surgeon at the Queen's Hospital and the inventor of a new form of surgical dressing; William Gilliver was secretary and later president of the trades council; T.H. Ryland was a manufacturer of nuts and bolts; Richard Peyton was a manufacturer of metal bedsteads; John Lewis was a manufacturer of bricks; James Hinks was a manufacturer of pens and a town councillor; Arthur Ryland was a solicitor and mayor in 1860-1.

[115] G.J. Johnson was a solicitor; Lawson Tait was a surgeon at the hospital for women; William Glydon was a manufacturer of metal tubes.

Isaac Horton was wont to say that George Dawson was the only man who talked common sense in the pulpit.[116]

It is thirty one years since Birmingham heard with a shock of intense grief that George Dawson was dead. Only two days before my brother had met him at New Street Station and noticed that he had a bad cough. "The old complaint", said Dawson, "It will soon be all right."

W.J. Clarke[117]

I date my first introduction to public work from the founding of the Perry Barr Institute, which was the first of the Birmingham suburban institutes, and of which I had the honour of being its chairman from its formation in 1872 until my resignation in 1882. Among those who lent valuable aid in connection with the founding and early struggles of the Institute was George Dawson and well do I remember the impression made on me by his handsome face and presence, his sincere and deeply-rooted piety, his simple and poetic eloquence, his courteous and considerate manners, his reverent demeanour when themes of sacred import were being discussed and kindly, though sometimes sarcastic, humour when lighter subjects were touched upon.

At that time the ordinary meetings of the Institute members were held in a house rented from the Rev. C.B. Snepp, the vicar of Perry Barr, conditionally on the church school room being placed at our disposal whenever a large audience might be expected. When, however, we applied for the use of it for a lecture at which George Dawson had kindly consented to give, it was emphatically refused.[118] The lecture was therefore given in the room connected with the Lozells chapel and it fell to my duty as chairman to explain to the audience the cause of our having to come so far from our own headquarters. I can recall not only the very words George

---

[116] Isaac Horton was a pork butcher with shops in the Bull Ring and across the Black Country.

[117] W.J. Clarke (d. 1913) served as a police officer and, in 1893, founded a charity in which the police provided clothing and boots to poor children. In its first year it distributed 1,064 pairs of boots and 3,773 items of clothing. This article was published in the *Birmingham Daily Gazette*, 18 July 1907.

[118] Like his father-in-law the brass manufacturer R.W. Winfield, Charles Busbridge Sneep an evangelical Tory.

Dawson used but his quietly and very effectively contemptuous manner in doing so. "With respect to what you have just heard", said he, "touching the reason of our coming here tonight, I have not the honour" - this with a significant shrug of the shoulders - "of knowing the reverend gentleman referred to. He appears, however, to know something about me, and very sorry I am that he does not like me. I have lectured before some of the most exclusive bodies in the kingdom - at Oxford, Cambridge, London and elsewhere - and I hope, therefore, with the aid of that patient resignation to the inevitable, which it becomes us all to cultivate, I shall manage to survive being shut out of the school room of the village of Perry Barr. However, this may be, all I can say is that if the vicar of this fortunate and enlightened place wants a battle in his parish, I am his man."

To refer to all the gifted men who lectured from the Institute platform, and to record the effect their sayings and doings produced in the homes of those members whose guests they usually became, would be impossible. However, I should like to mention Edward Capern, the postman-poet. Capern was a singularly genial and pleasant companion, whose custom it was to recite in the homes of his friends his patriotic and stirring poems with a fire and fervour which sometimes alarmed them and the more touching of his pastoral and domestic poems with a pathetic tenderness which would draw tears to their eyes.[119]

The Perry Barr Institute was followed by the opening of a similar institute for Edgbaston and Harborne and others for Moseley and King's Heath, Acocks Green, Yardley, Sutton Coldfield, Wednesbury and Leamington and other districts, most of them federated in the Suburban Institutes' Union, of which I had the honour of being the first chairman.

---

[119] Edward Capern achieved great fame as the Devon postman who wrote poetry. When he retired, he moved to Birmingham, living in Harborne.

Sir William Cook[120]

When I entered the municipal assembly in 1872 Birmingham was under the domination of a party who called themselves the 'economists'. Its leaders numbered Sadler, Biggs, Cornforth and Brinsley, who all leaned towards Conservatism.[121] At that time I had not attached myself to party politics, and it has always been interesting to myself, and those about me, to recall the circumstances of my first election to the council. I had been brought into prominence, as it seemed, by reason of long service at the Severn Street adult school, having been secretary to White's large class for nearly twenty years.[122] I remember being at work about noon one day when a deputation called on me with an intimation that they had heard a good account of me in connection with the Severn Street school and they wanted to know if I could become a candidate in Hampton ward. The upshot was that the next evening found me addressing a meeting in the Barr Street recreation room and opposing a candidate who had already spent seventeen years on the council. I was elected by a majority of over three hundred and was never afterwards opposed in my municipal career.[123] Although then unattached to politics, my main supporters were J.S. Wright and his friends and the contest was really of a political nature. The elections of the following year entirely altered the aspect of things and changed the operations of the council, the regime of the so-called 'economists' being at an end and we found ourselves at the commencement of the Chamberlain era.

At the time of my entrance to the council, there was no sanitary committee in existence. Scarlet fever and other infections

---

[120] Sir William Cook (1834- 1908) was a manufacturer of pins. For over thirty years he served as the chairman of the sanitary committee in Birmingham and this work led, in 1906, to a knighthood. He was briefly MP for East Birmingham but ousted because he did not toe the Chamberlain line over Irish Home Rule. This article was published in the *Birmingham Daily Gazette,* 5 September 1907.

[121] John Sadler was secretary of the Birmingham Gas Company and chairman of the public works committee. Ambrose Biggs was a manufacturer of tobacco products. John Cornforth was a manufacturer of screws and nails.

[122] William White was a printer who, in 1848, became heavily involved in this school, which had been established a few years earlier by Quakers. He eventually presided over 200 working men. (There was a separate school of women). Later elected to the council, White was a key ally of Chamberlain.

[123] Cook 1,019; Tonks 705. Samuel Tonks was a manufacturer of tin plate.

were very rife in Birmingham and the necessity for a sanitary authority to devote itself to the consideration of the health of the town was pressing. A sanitary committee was appointed and on this committee I was placed, and, within a year or two, I was elected chairman. Questions of public health were so pressing and serious that the committee met weekly and it was very exceptional for Chamberlain to be absent. The question of appointing ward inspectors was early brought forward and the committee also asked the council to empower them to put on labouring men to whitewash the courts and alleys in the lower part of the town. In these matters influential support was accorded us, Henry Hawkes being a staunch advocate of our policy, saying that it was no use having a sanitary committee unless they were given the tools to work with.[124] The opposing party strongly objected to the appointment of inspectors, describing the proposal as 'un-English and an invasion of the sanctities of domestic life.' Despite all opposition, the inspectors and whitewashers were engaged.

One or two violent outbreaks of smallpox led to the decision to provide a hospital in which to isolate and treat that dread disease. The committee experienced considerable difficulty in this, however, for wherever they sought to secure a site there was a great outcry. They ultimately procured a piece of land which had been occupied by the Poor Law authorities for the purpose of treating their own pauper patients suffering from smallpox. This was taken over by the sanitary committee, who there made provision for dealing with small pox as far as concerned the whole population of the borough. Then the Lodge Road hospital was provided for the treatment of scarlet fever, and further hospital accommodation was provided by the acquisition of a site in Yardley Road.

About the time I joined the council the sewage question had reached a serious stage. Injunctions had been obtained against the town in respect to the disposal of sewage at Saltley and it was absolutely necessary that some steps of a preventative nature should be taken. This led to the establishment of the privy-pan system.[125] One of my recollections of working on the sanitary committee is

---

[124] Hawkes was appointed coroner in Birmingham in 1875. He charged 26s 8d per inquest.
[125] Pans were placed under each privy seat in poorer parts of the town. They were emptied each week.

that when, at one of the meetings at which thanks were accorded to the chairman, and the clerk had drafted the customary resolution to that effect, Chamberlain smilingly remarked that that was 'not full enough' and himself drew up another resolution.

Frank Wright[126]

At the first meeting of the Birmingham Liberal Association which I ever attended, I was a visitor and not yet a member. That was in 1868 and the Association was occupied with choosing a third Member of Parliament for the borough. My father was proposed, but withdrew his name and recommended to his friends the name of William Radford as a working man's representative. Ultimately P.H. Muntz was selected.

I remember a meeting in the town hall in 1869 at which Thomas Lloyd moved, and Joseph Chamberlain seconded, a resolution approving of the Irish Church Bill.[127] They were but imperfectly heard, but Sampson Lloyd, who moved an amendment, was not heard at all. He declared he would be heard if he stayed all day and all night. I think it was held at midday. He stood up for quite an hour and then gave way. The resolution was put and declared carried. There was a scene of the wildest confusion. Prize fighters – they were not uncommon in those days – jumped over the side gallery to the floor of the hall and fought right and left with metal knuckledusters. I saw blood flow, and then thought it was time to go home.

From 1874 to 1884 I was a member of the town council and my colleague in the representation of St. Stephen's ward was Richard Chamberlain. In those days the council consisted of three Chamberlains – Joseph, Arthur and Richard – and they were days when the level of municipal oratory stood high.[128] Of course, Joseph

---

[126] Frank Wright (1853-1922) was the son of the Liberal stalwart John Skirrow Wright. He was 'a commanding personality and as a political fighter ... hard-hitting'. In December 1900 he was with Lloyd George on the platform at the town hall when the audience sought to forcibly end the meeting. Obit. *Birmingham Daily Gazette,* 13 June 1922. This article was published in the *Birmingham Daily Gazette,* 13 July 1907.

[127] Thomas Lloyd was the defeated Liberal candidate in Bewdley in 1868. See ibid., 15 June 1869 for a full account of this meeting.

[128] Arthur and Richard were the brothers of Joseph Chamberlain.

Chamberlain was easily first, but Alderman Hawkes was always a brilliant talker and Alderman Avery also made good speeches - perhaps a little old fashioned and ponderous but always able.[129] Other good speakers I remember were Sir Thomas Martineau, Aldermen Powell Williams and Sadler and last, but not least, C.E. Matthews.[130] I was a member of the gas, free libraries and lunatic asylum committees and, during my membership of the latter body, the Rubery Hall Asylum was built. Another event of that period was the burning of the free library during which my father had a narrow escape from death through the falling debris while he was helping to rescue the books.[131] Three election contests, and one election petition from which I came out acquitted of all charges, form a municipal experience at least interesting, not to say exciting, in character.

An interesting experience befell me when, in 1876, I was on a business visit to the United States. I was at the same time the bearer of a resolution which the town council had passed congratulating the Americans on the centennial celebration of the declaration of independence. This was presented in the form of an illuminated address which I handed to President Grant. The latter struck me as a very courteous man, of gentle bearing but very reticent of speech. Two years later he visited Birmingham and I was secretary of the reception committee. He was entertained at a banquet at the town hall and was also a guest at a private dinner party which Mr Chamberlain gave in his honour. I remember one of the guests remarking of the President that there 'didn't seem to be much too him.' Upon that our host observed that that was what had struck him with regard to many famous men he had met.[132]

If it not be out of place to say it here, I pride myself on three things in my political experience - that I have been elected by my local friends three times to be president of the Liberal Association, that I have been chosen sixteen times to be one of the twenty four members of the National Liberal Federation executive and that I

---

[129] Thomas Avery was a Tory councillor; his family manufactured scales.
[130] Sir Thomas Martineau was a solicitor and was mayor in 1886-7. Joseph Powell Williams was a councillor for thirteen years and MP for South Birmingham for nineteen years. He was a central figure in Chamberlain's operation. See A. Reekes, *The Birmingham Political Machine*, pp. 95-7, 146-9.
[131] See *Birmingham Daily Post,* 13 January 1879.
[132] See ibid., 18 October 1877.

was hon. secretary to the Transvaal committee to protest against the country being led to into the South African war.

William McGregor[133]

When I first came to Birmingham in 1870 the Franco-Prussian war was creating a boom worth remembering. Everybody seemed to be in the gun trade and money was plentiful with the working classes. Heads of families earned five pounds a week and more and even the women in many instances were getting quite as much, particularly if they understood rifle-browning. Labour was so scarce that frocks were frequently offered as presents to young women and girls if they would go and work in cartridge factories. The japanning trade was also very good at that point and female labour in that branch of local industry was well rewarded. As a consequence the expenditure was on a liberal scale likewise and scarlet and black plaid shawls used to sell freely at as much as half a sovereign each and Paisley shawls would fetch three guineas. As I first knew Birmingham, it was the aspiration of the working man to save up enough money to take to a public house business, while those a little higher in the social scale were putting their savings into property. Few people kept banking accounts, not even among those who were doing an extensive business. I do not remember that there was one branch bank outside the centre of town.

As a Scot and a new arrival I came across some curious samples of ignorance concerning my native land. When board schools were first instituted, the dearth of teachers led to numbers, particularly female teachers, being imported from Scotland and George Dawson, in a famous speech, raised an objection on account of their accent. Yet George Dawson was a Master of Arts of Glasgow University! At the time of starting my business, Summer Lane was a very busy thoroughfare. A great number of manufacturers and tradesmen lived on their business premises. With the appearance of the Harding Street gang, ruffianism became

---

[133] William McGregor (1847-1911) was the founder of the Football League in 1888. He was closely associated with Aston Villa and the draper's shop he ran with his brother Peter stocked football shirts and shorts and became a place for fans to meet. There is an entry for him in the *ODNB*. This article was published in the *Birmingham Daily Gazette,* 19 September 1907.

so rampant that the lower end of Summer Lane became a very dangerous quarter.[134] It was no uncommon thing for the police to be stoned and severely handled. The pearl button district was also the centre of the boxing fraternity, professional and amateur, and Tom Hill, Billy Shillcock, amateur champions, and Jim Carney and other well-known professionals were the heroes of this neighbourhood.[135]

I recall the higgledy-piggledy aspect of the streets – houses seemed to be planted anywhere and anyhow. There were no shop holidays then, though people readily knocked off work for such occasions as the races at Sutton or occasional fetes at Aston Lower Grounds. The male portion of the working class went about Sunday and Saturday in the same attire. Overcoats were worn summer and winter. It was no uncommon thing to see batches of workmen standing at street corners with dirty aprons all hours of the day.

My earliest recollection of football dates back to boyhood in the country village which was my home near the Roman camp of Ardoch in Perthshire. A mansion was being built twenty miles away and thither the stone was carted from the railway station near my native village after being dressed. Many masons were therefore working in the vicinity and they had brought with them a football. Sometimes the village youngsters joined in the game, but more often we played with the ball when the masons were at work. It was a very rude and rough game, played without rules of any kind, and its crudity may be imagined when I mention that he who kicked highest was deemed the best player.

From those boyish days I never saw a football again until I came to Birmingham. This was somewhere about 1875, when my brother came home one day and said he had seen a game of football on the Bristol Road. Already I was taking an interest, at a distance, in the doings of the Queen's park club and, by working my half-holiday round to Saturday and arranging to return to business at six o'clock, I managed to get off to see a game for

---

[134] The Harding Street gang practised pick-pocketing and robbery. See *Birmingham Daily Post,* 26 April 1880 for the imprisonment of one of their number, sixteen-year old Samuel Everall.
[135] Tom Hill was featherweight champion of England. Jim Craney was a prize fighter: see ibid, 8 October 1881, for his two-hour long bout with Jimmy Ireland which ended with him being 'shockingly cut about the face' and arrested.

myself. The Calthorpe was the leading club in Birmingham and they played on a field at Bournbrook.[136] Then I heard of Aston Villa as being a small club with three Scotsmen in its ranks – the two Lindsays and George Ramsay.[137] Archie Hunter was the next Scot to join and from that time I became a member and, in 1878, was made vice-president. There was also the Birmingham club which played at the Lower Grounds and was often called 'the Quilters' because the two young Quilters were prominent members. This club was addicted to much unpunctuality, matches advertised to commence at 3 or 3.30 often not beginning till half an hour later. I sent a letter to the local papers protesting against this late kick-off – so that I was the first to write a letter of complaint against a football club.[138]

Simeon Doggett[139]

Always actively identified with the Conservative cause, I found that our side of politics was very much in the shade and it took some amount of moral, and occasionally physical, courage to proclaim oneself an adherent of the Conservative Party. In those days I lived in Leopold Street and soon became connected with the Conservative organisation in Deritend ward. The chairman of our ward was Frank Smith and J.B. Stone was the president of the Conservative Association – the office now held by Sir Francis Lowe, who is, in my opinion, a born leader of men.[140] The younger spirits among us in Deritend determined to start a working men's club, and its headquarters at the outset were placed at John Allen's licensed house in Ravenhurst Street, Allen himself being a noted Conservative in the district.

---

[136] Founded in 1873, the club took its name from Calthorpe Park but soon moved to a ground behind the Bournbrook Hotel.

[137] William and James Lindsay; born in Golspie in Sutherland, they were ironmongers. George Ramsay and Archie Hunter both served as captains of Aston Villa.

[138] H.G. Quilter was manager of the Aston Lower Grounds Company. This business failed in February 1881.

[139] This article was published in the *Birmingham Daily Gazette,* 31 January 1908.

[140] See *Birmingham Daily Post,* 11 December 1884 for a report of a meeting of the Deritend Conservative Association, chaired by Smith. 'There was not a large attendance. A number of seats were reserved at a charge of 6d', the paper took pleasure in reporting.

A memorable gathering in the early days of the Deritend club was that attended by Lord Calthorpe, Lord Randolph Churchill and Colonel Fred Burnaby, with Mr Muntz accompanying them.[141] I remember that we marched from Allen's to a hall in Chandos Road and, as we went on our way, with Colonel Burnaby in the middle of us, the radicals climbed on the banks and walls at the side and slung bags of flour atop of us till we looked like a straggling procession of dusty millers! The Deritend club gained favour and support to such an extent that a desire next found expression that we should have a place of our own. At the corner of Angelina Street and Upper Highgate Street stood some premises called the Tower, which had been a beer house. These we rented and our membership grew till it reached upwards of 300 in number. The club was equipped with bagatelle and cards and other games, and later with a billiard table. We made rapid progress and after four or five years found it necessary to remove to other premises in Moseley Road.

A feature of this Deritend political institution was the enthusiasm with which workers were ready at election times. I remember the general election of 1880 – there was some fun then! I remember seeing Colonel Burnaby at a meeting in Smith Street, when the process of ejection was continuous. The Colonel sat on the platform, coolly lighted his pipe, and waited in calm and good-humoured contentment till something like order was restored. A fine fellow was Colonel Burnaby, an Englishman from the crown of his head to the soles of his feet, genial, kind, good-tempered, an enthusiastic Conservative, a good speaker and a plucky fighter – a man, in short, who was not to be turned aside by any obstacle, small or great.

Birmingham Conservatism was inspired and vitalised by a remarkable degree in those days. The rank and file of the party were ready to follow men like Burnaby and Lord Randolph Churchill anywhere. My memories of Lord Randolph are clear and fixed. He was a very brilliant man, full of energy, zeal and 'go'; he was talented, crisp and attracting as an orator. I recollect being present at a great town hall meeting, where Lord Randolph Churchill held a huge assembly spell-bound for an hour or more.

---

[141] Burnaby and Calthorpe were the Tory candidates in Birmingham in 1880. See S. Roberts and R. Ward, *Mocking Men of Power. Comic Art in Birmingham 1861-1911*, (Birmingham, 2014), pp. 26-7, 48-51.

The radicals were well in evidence inside the hall, but there was no disturbance. Lady Randolph sat at her husband's side and handed up to him his notes on little scraps of paper.

The first Conservative member whom I helped return to the town council was George Beard, an iron master at the Cape, Smethwick. Brinsley and Sadler, who were at the time influential figures in the town council, wished that Beard's name be withdrawn, but the more persistent of us were bent on a fight and a good one was made on Beard's behalf against Ephraim Gooch.[142] So effective was this display of militant Conservatism that, when Rotton Park was constituted a ward a year or so later, Beard was one of the first members chosen for the new ward.[143] I remember a stout contest in South Birmingham in the general election of 1885 between Joseph Powell Williams and Henry Hawkes. The rain fell in torrents all day. I was asked to bring up some lady workers and, when I came up with a bevy of enthusiastic fair ones, Hawkes, glancing pathetically at the rain and then at the ladies, observed, "They shan't go out – I would rather lose the seat ten times over than see ladies go out on such a day!" But the ladies went and helped Hawkes make a splendid fight of it, though he did not win the seat for Powell Williams carried too many guns for him.[144]

Sir Francis Lowe[145]

On leaving King Edward's School the law, in the person of my father, who was a solicitor in Birmingham, claimed me and I accordingly served my articles with him and in due course became a qualified solicitor myself. The debates at the Law Students' Society early attracted me and I gained my first experience in speech-making and acquired a liking for it. I acquired valuable practice as a debater with the Law Students, practice which I improved by subsequent membership of the Birmingham and Edgbaston Debating Society, of which I filled the various offices and in due course became its president. On one occasion I led the affirmative

---

[142] This was in 1872: Gooch 1,707; Beard, 782.
[143] Beard, 1,148; Hadley, 854.
[144] Williams 5,099; Hawkes, 3,311.
[145] Sir Francis Lowe (1852-1929) was a solicitor who represented Edgbaston from 1898 until 1929. He was knighted in 1905. This article was published in the *Birmingham Daily Gazette,* 13 June 1907.

on a resolution for reform in the administration of the town council which, in my opinion, was conducted in far too one-sided a fashion, with the result that most of its business was cut and dried beforehand and did not receive as much criticism and discussion as I thought desirable in the public interest. I managed to carry the resolution with a considerable majority.

My first venture into public affairs was made when, in conjunction with Henry Lakin Smith, I helped to found the Municipal Reform Association.[146] We ran a couple of candidates at the municipal elections, but both were defeated. The fact of the Association being run on non-political lines contributed to our falling between two stools so that we were able to do little good. Accordingly I associated myself with the Conservative cause – I had generally taken a leading part on the Conservative side in all political debates with the Edgbaston Society – and became chairman of the Ladywood organisation and next came forward as a candidate for St. Thomas' ward. Although it was a radical ward, I managed to win the seat owing to a split on the other side and I sat in the council for the next three years.[147]

When I came up for re-election in November 1885, we were in the throes of a general election. Lord Randolph Churchill was attacking John Bright in the Central Division, of which St. Thomas' ward was part; and I was at the same time Conservative candidate in East Birmingham. It was in a way only an affair of outposts, but extraordinarily keen and exciting and Lord Randolph Churchill came down to Bristol Street board school and spoke at a meeting at which I occupied the chair. In the event I was defeated by about 200 votes, but the poll made a very favourable comparison with Lord Randolph's poll in the Central Division. This and the East Birmingham contest in which I was involved in at the same time were certainly amongst the most arduous of my political experiences.[148]

East Birmingham, when I contested it, was absolutely without organisation on the Conservative side and, as there were contests going on in all the other divisions, we could not, of course, get any

---

[146] Lakin Smith was a fellow solicitor. His attempts to get elected to the town council as an independent always ended in failure: in Rotton Park in November 1883 he secured only 93 votes.
[147] 1882 result: Lowe, 1,116; Jerrett, 1,036.
[148] Cook, 4,277; Lowe, 3,025. Cook's majority was in fact 1,252.

outside help. This meant a very uphill fight, but we polled remarkably well under the circumstances. When the Liberal split came about in 1886, my party asked me to stand for East Birmingham again and I should have been adopted as the candidate but for representatives reaching us from London that it was desired to put up Henry Matthews for the division. Therefore I stood aside and took the chair at Matthews' first meeting. He was duly elected and immediately afterwards became Home Secretary. In November of that year I was chosen as one of Duddeston's representatives on the town council and sat for another three years.[149]

Now I come to relate what was certainly one of the most unpleasant of my experiences. It arose on account of the very just claims of the Conservatives of Birmingham that they were by virtue of their numbers and strength in the city entitled to a larger share of parliamentary representation. On the death of George Dixon the right to nominate the Unionist candidate for the Edgbaston vacancy was, after some difficulty, conceded to the Conservatives and they unanimously invited me to become their candidate. There was subsequently a good deal of unpleasant controversy with the Liberal Unionist committee, but I was eventually returned without opposition.

Edward Taylor[150]

I entered upon my chosen vocation by becoming the first student in the School of Art at Burslem. The Burslem School was held in a low room situate in the yard of the Legs of Man Inn and W.J. Muckley, an old Birmingham student, was the art master.[151] From the Burslem School I passed on as a student in training at South Kensington. I have a memory of seeing the Great Exhibition of

---

[149] Lowe, 1,169; Barber, 1,045; Edmonds, 84. Edmonds was brought forward by the Birmingham Working Men's Radical Association.

[150] Edward Taylor (1838-1912) was headmaster of the School of Art. When he retired, he was presented with an armchair and a bookcase stocked with books. This article was published in the *Birmingham Daily Gazette,* 7 December 1907.

[151] William Jabez Muckley began life as a glass engraver and his work was much-admired at the Great Exhibition. He won a scholarship to the School of Art in Birmingham and was headmaster of the School of Art in Burslem from 1853 until 1858.

1851. I visibly remember the glass fountain made by Follett & Clarkson Osler and that trees were inside the building and, by ascending to the galleries, one could get among the upper branches with the sparrows flying about.

In 1852 I obtained the appointment of headmaster of the newly-provided School of Art at Lincoln and at the beautiful cathedral city I remained for thirteen years or so. When I was at Lincoln, I thought of being an art teacher only, but a mere incident led me to work of a more individual nature. The honorary secretary of the Art School was a cathedral canon and also an amateur painter. I was out with him one day when I happened to notice a fine old man and at once exclaimed that I should like to paint him. 'Well', said the canon, 'he is one of my parishioners and I'll get him to sit for you.' I finished the picture and sent it to the Royal Academy. Imagine my delight to find that the picture was accepted. Other pictures that I have exhibited at the Royal Academy were 'Nearing Home', a life-size picture of sailors looking out of the porthole of a man-of-war, which was engraved in the *Graphic* with an extract from a very favourable press notice of the picture by W.M. Rossetti; 'The Cloister Well', a large picture of Lincoln Cathedral; 'Twas a famous victory', painted in the Midland Institute from a few hours' sketch in the National Gallery, the caretaker of the Institute sitting for the veteran; and several landscapes.

My subsequent associations with art work in Birmingham had quite an accidental beginning. I was a member of the Hogarth Club and, while there one evening, Wilmot Pilsbury, the well-known member of the Royal Watercolour Society, himself a Birmingham man, asked if I was going in for the art headmastership in Birmingham, which had been vacant for a year, but of which I had not heard.[152] I did so and received the appointment in 1876. Coming to Birmingham to take up my work in what was, I think, the oldest school of art in the country, I never suspected but that the school was accommodated in a good building. Instead I found it housed in the top room of the Midland Institute. To reach it was an awful climb up four or five flights of stairs and the place itself was ill-lighted. I told John Henry Chamberlain, who was chairman, that we

---

[152] The Hogarth Club, founded in 1858, was meeting place for painters who were in sympathy with Pre-Raphaelite art. Wilmot Pilsbury was a product of the School of Art in Birmingham and painted landscapes.

must get a new school, but his reply was that so little was the interest locally taken in art education that we should not get five pounds towards the cost. Then there came a period of enlargements at the Institute and the School of Art had to make the best of temporary quarters in the top rooms of the council house and even about the corridors.

When we went back to the Institute, we had little more room and the place was still dreadfully crowded and inadequate. Then I met by appointment Sir Richard Tangye at a memorable conversazione of the Royal Society of Artists and had a long conversation with him.[153] All my friends thought I was selling him pictures, but we were discussing something of much more importance. He asked me not to mention anything of what he had said as he and his brother George Tangye promised to do something first for the art gallery. It was sometime later when Sir Richard announced his proposals relative to the School of Art. Thus came about the building of the new School, William Barwick Cregoe-Colmore giving the land. The number of students increased and additions to the Art School were made. Among its early students were Walter Langley and W.F. Wainwright and many others who have since obtained distinction.[154]

When I reached the age of sixty five my time for retirement came and the last day of my headmastership, with all its happy surprises and warmth of good wishes from masters and students, is among the best of my memories. Since my retirement I have acted as art examiner for South Kensington and have turned, with my son, my attention to the making of Ruskin pottery. My father was an earthenware manufacturer at Hanley and in my youth therefore I had seen something of the potter's craft. The shapes are all made on the potter's wheel, all decorated by hand, and the painting is all in and under the glaze, except the lustre, while only leadless glazes are used.

---

[153] S. Roberts, *Sir Richard Tangye: A Cornish Entrepreneur in Victorian Birmingham*, (Birmingham, 2015), pp. 28-9.
[154] Walter Langley and William John Wainwright both had connections with Newlyn. Langley settled there, but Wainwright sent most of his life in Birmingham.

Illustrations

1. John Angell James. Pastor at the Congregationalist chapel in Carr's Lane, he was very highly regarded as a preacher. His theological writings also enjoyed excellent sales.

ILLUSTRATIONS

2. Samuel Timmins addressing a meeting. The reporters can be seen making notes. Also depicted, from left to right, are R.W. Dale, J.S. Wright and George Dixon.

3. John Skirrow Wright. A manufacturer of military buttons, he played a pivotal role in establishing Liberal dominance in Birmingham.

ILLUSTRATIONS

4. The Hope and Anchor in Navigation Street. For many years this was the venue for Sunday evening debates organised by the working class politicians of the town.

5. The Murphy riots of June 1867. Police and soldiers in Park Street, where serious clashes took place between the supporters of the Protestant lecturer and Irish Catholics.

6. W.J. Davis. A doughty defender of his trade and, as a councillor, of working people in Birmingham.

7. Lawson Tait, a pioneering surgeon at the hospital for women, was a member of George Dawson's Church of the Saviour. He is depicted sitting on a pan cart, which was used to empty privies.

8. The statue of George Dawson unveiled five years after his death in October 1881 did not meet with local approval and had to be replaced.

9. The *Birmingham Daily Post* was deluged with letters criticising the statue, which at first it declined to print. The main complaint was that the statue bore little resemblance to Dawson.

10. W.J. Cook. For over thirty years, he presided over public health improvements in Birmingham.

11. C.A. Vince. A Liberal Unionist organiser, he was a key ally of Joseph Chamberlain.

12. William McGregor. A draper associated with Aston Villa, he was, in 1888, the founder of the Football League.

13. Sir Francis Lowe. A solicitor, he became the leading local champion of the Tory cause.

14. Sir Richard Tangye. A self-made man, he put up half the funds needed to build the School of Art.

WHO GETS THE PROFIT?

MR. RICHARD TANGYE.—Look here, Mr. Cobbles, you've no right to filch sixty per cent. from the Public because the poor miners have got a miserable rise of ten per cent.

15. Never afraid of putting the cat amongst the pigeons, Tangye publicly condemned the coal dealers in November 1888 for what he regarded as an exorbitant increase in their prices.

Index

Acland, T.D.	38
Allday, Joseph	41
Aston, John	12, 24
Aston Villa	55-7
Attwood, Thomas	1, 4, 42, 44-5
Avery, Thomas	54
Ball, Edward	45
Barrett, J.C.	iv, 16, 23, 33
Bingley House	20, 32
Brassworkers	39-40
Breese, C.S.	15
Bright, John	6, 29, 34-5, 38, 44, 60
Brinsley, William	41, 51, 59
Bristow, Edward	7
Brookfields demonstrations	29, 35, 45
Bull Ring riots	iv, 2, 5-6, 10
Burnaby, Frederick	58
Burritt, Elihu	23-4
Capern, Edward	50
Chamberlain, J.H.	47-8, 62
Chamberlain, Joseph	iv, 37, 41-2, 44, 511, 53-4
Churchill, Lord Randolph	58-60
Cock-staking	31-2
Cook, William	37, 42, 73
Craney, Jim	56
Crimean War	28, 30, 34, 38
Crompton, Sarah	45
Dalzell, Allen	28-9
Daly, John	29
Davis, W.J.	v, 69
Dawson, George	12, 17, 20, 45-50, 55, 71-2
Day, James	19-20
Deeley, John	v
Dickinson, Alfred	iii
Dixon, George	6, 25, 29, 35-6, 40, 61, 65
Dog fighting	11, 31

INDEX

East, Timothy	33
Eateries	20-1
Edmonds, George	iv, 3, 8
Edmonds, Robert	28
Education	4-5, 7, 13, 33
Evans, Sebastian	35, 48
Fairs	21-2
Finnemore, Joseph	12
Football	56-7
Freemasonry	1
Gamgee, J.S.	48
Gilliver, William	48
Gladstone, W.E.	36
Hack, Henry	iii
Hall, Billy	10
Harding Street gang	55-6
Harris, William	35-6
Hawkes, Henry	52-3, 59
Hazelwood House	33
Heaton, Ralph	39
Hill, Tom	56
Hollins, Daniel	19
Hollins, Peter	19
Hope & Anchor	28, 67
Horton, Isaac	49
Hutton, Hugh	1
Jabet, George	22
James, John Angell	14, 16, 33-4, 64
King Edward's School	4, 13, 59
King, Thomas	27
Langley, Walter	63
Lee, J. Prince	13
Lind, Jenny	15-16
Lines, Samuel	19
Lloyd, Sampson	35, 53
Lowe, Sir Francis	57

INDEX

Manufacturing	12-13
Martineau, Sir Thomas	54
Matthews, Henry	61
Mellon, Alfred	26
Mendelssohn, F.	26
Middlemore, J.T.	iii
Morton, Samuel	28
Muckley, W.J.	61
Muntz, G.F.	3, 12, 29
Muntz, P.H.	33, 36, 53, 58
Murphy riots	16
Newhall Hill meetings	iv, 1, 3-4
Oliver, J.W.	45
Omnibuses	21, 42-3
Palmer, John	29-30
Pigeon-flying	31
Police	10-11, 47
Powell Williams, J.	59
Prize-fighting	10-11
Public health	40, 51-3
Quilter, H.G.	57
Racing	32
Ragg, Thomas	24-5
Railways	3, 30
Raphall, M.J.	5
Ratting	32
Ryland, Arthur	48
Sadler, John	51
Scholefield, Joshua	4
Shakespeare, William	21, 27
Shaw, George	4-5
Sherlock, Father	25, 34
Simpson, Mercer	26-7
Smith, Frank	57
Smith, H.L.	57
Sneep, C.S.	49

Spooner, Richard	iv, 24, 42
Stone, J.B.	57
Sturge, Charles	6
Sturge, Joseph	6
Tait, R. Lawson	48, 70
Tangye, Richard	63, 77-8
Taylor, James	36
Theatre	19-20, 25-6
Tilley, Vesta	27
Timmins, Samuel	16, 20, 47, 65
Townsend, Edward	iii
Tripe eating	8, 17-18
Underhill, Richard	18
Vaughan, Robert	17
Victoria, Queen	14-15
Vince, Charles	43-4
Wainwright, W.F.	63
Westley Richards	12-14
Westwood, John	8, 22-3
Whateley, James	37
Whateley, John	30
White, William	51
Wilson, John	22
Wombell's menagerie	22
Woodman public house	8, 23
Wright, J.S.	iv, 29-30, 35-6, 38, 44, 51, 53, 65-6

About the Author

Stephen Roberts is an Honorary Associate Professor at the Research School of Humanities and the Arts in the Australian National University and an Honorary Fellow of the Shakespeare Institute in the University of Birmingham.

THE BIRMINGHAM BIOGRAPHIES SERIES

Already published:

Dr J.A. Langford 1823-1903: A Self-Taught Working Man and the Sale of American Degrees in Victorian Britain. 65 pp, 8 photographs, 2014. ISBN: 978 1495475122. £5.99.

Sir Benjamin Stone 1838-1914: Photographer, Traveller and Politician. 102 pp, 20 photographs, 2014. ISBN: 978 1499265521. £7.99.

Mocking Men of Power: Comic Art in Birmingham 1861-1914. 60 cartoons, 2014. ISBN: 978 1502764560. £8.99. (with Roger Ward)

Sir Richard Tangye 1833-1906: A Cornish Entrepreneur in Victorian Birmingham. 65 pp, 2015. ISBN: 978-1512207910. £4.99.

Joseph Chamberlain's Highbury: A Very Public Private House, 44pp, 2015. ISBN: 978-1515044680. £3.99.

Now Mr Editor!: Letters to the Newspapers of Nineteenth Century Birmingham. 100 pp, 2015, ISBN: 978-1518685897. £6.99.

Joseph Gillott: And Four Other Birmingham Manufacturers 1784-1892. 98 pp, 2016. ISBN: 1539483069. £6.99.

Birmingham 1889: One year in a Victorian City. 86 pp. 2017, ISBN 978-1544139227. £4.99.

About the Author

James Whateley and the Survival of Chartism. 63pp, 2018, ISBN:978-1983503030. £4.99

These books can be ordered from Amazon and other booksellers.

Printed in Great Britain
by Amazon